ナルト

The NARUTO SAGA

The Unofficial Guide

cocoro books

Published by DH Publishing, Inc.
1-20-2-518 Higashi Ikebukuro, Toshima-Ku
Tokyo 170-0013, Japan
http://www.dhp-online.com
cocoro books is an imprint of DH Publishing, Inc.

First Published 2006
Second Published 2007

Text and illustrations©2006 by DH Publishing, Inc.

Printed in CHINA

Printed by Miyuki Inter-Media Hong Kong, Inc.
Compiled by Kazuhisa Fujie, Matthew Lane and Walt Wyman
Publisher: Hiroshi Yokoi
Design: Kazuhisa Fujie
Editor: Kazuhisa Fujie
ISBN 1-932897-16-X
EAN 978-1-932897-16-6
By courtesy of Akio Kurono(cac co,ltd.)

The Naruto Saga

How to Use
In this book, the eighth in the popular Mysteries and Secrets Revealed! series, you'll find everything you need to know about Naruto and much more! And it's so easy to use…just follow the Naruto code below and within a few hours you will be a Jonin-level expert!

Questions and Answers
Want to find out why who did what when and where? Then this is the book for you. Includes 73 questions and detailed answers on every Naruto topic, from fighting techniques to character backgrounds and history.

Glossary
When you speak the lingo everything is so much easier. At the back of this book you will find all of the characters that make an appearance in the first part of the series along with a comprehensive list of Ninja techniques.

Keyword Index
Want to go straight to Konohagakure Ninja Academy? Then start at the alphabetical Keyword Index at the back of the book. There you'll find page links to every destination, character and Ninja technique in Naruto's world.

A Note on Translations
In most cases the translation for Ninja techniques and weapons etc. are romanized versions of the original Japanese, with either a literal translation of the Kanji in brackets or occasionally the Viz manga translations. Character names appear in Japanese style, with last names first.

Series Overview

Naruto was first serialized in Shueisha's weekly Shonen Jump magazine in 1999 and continues to run even to this day. In the US, Viz Media have been publishing the manga series in English and, at the time of writing, are just about to release vol 11 (the book form of the manga is in its 34th volume in Japan). The Japanese manga spawned a highly successful anime spin-off. The English-version of the anime was first aired in the States in 2005 on Cartoon Network's Toonami and then on Canada's YTV soon afterwards. The show is also broadcast in the UK by Jetix, and will be making its debut in Australia and New Zealand this year (2006) on Cartoon Network. In addition, three feature-length Naruto movies have been made, as well as numerous Naruto games produced for various different consoles. The first English versions of the games, Naruto: Clash of the Ninja and Naruto: Ninja Council, were released earlier this year on the Nintendo Gamecube and Gameboy respectively.

While Naruto's international success has undoubtedly been fuelled by the anime, games, movies and various other merchandise on the market, this book considers the original Japanese manga to be the definitive work. As such, all the explanations and names of techniques in this book are based on the version of Naruto published in Japan by Shueisha.

CONTENTS

The NARUTO SAGA

PART01

NINJA's Secrets

01 *What are the Five Great Countries in the Naruto series?*

Naruto is from the village of Konohagakure which is in the Land of Fire. On the same continent as the Land of Fire there are several other countries of various different sizes. Of these, the biggest are the Land of Wind, Land of Earth, Land of Lightning and Land of Water. Along with the Land of Fire they make up the Five Great Countries. Each of these five countries has military strength in the form of Shinobi (Ninja) Villages. The Land of Fire is characterized by the gentle, rolling hills which spread across its vast land mass. It is rich in arable land and has a large population, so is an economically prosperous country. Because it is located in the center of the continent, it has played a historical role as an important trade and transport route for other countries and has been influenced by the mix of different cultures passing through. The village of Konohagakure is the main Ninja village in the Land of Fire. Because of this, the head Ninja from the village has for generations been known as Lord Hokage ("Hokage" literally translates as "Fire

Shadow").

The Land of Earth is dominated by its desolate, rocky terrain, which acts as a natural fortress. The main Ninja village in this country is the village of Iwagakure and the head Ninja is known as Tsuchikage (Earth Shadow).

Occupying a vast area, the Land of Wind is mainly desert and has a very low annual rate of rainfall. Most of the population is concentrated in settlements built next to the oases dotted throughout the land. Despite the harsh environment, the population is surprisingly large. The main Ninja village in this country is the village of Sunagakure. The leader of the village goes by the name of Kazegake (Wind Shadow).

The Land of Water is an island detached from the mainland of the continent. It is a mountainous country surrounded by lots of small islands, each with its own people and cultures. This country is host to the Ninja village of Kirigakure. The top Ninja in this village is called Mizugake (Water Shadow).

The last of the five countries is the Land of Lightning, whose name derives from the crashing sound of thunder which echos throughout its mountain ranges. The country is home to numerous natural hot spring resorts, as well as the Ninja village of Kumogakure. The head of this village is known as Raikage (Lightning Shadow).

In addition to these villages there are some other, smaller Ninja villages (Otogakure, Ryugakure, Kusagakure and Amegakure). In general though, the Ninja trained in these villages do not match up to the Ninja from the main Shinobi villages in the Five Great Countries. The title of Kage (Shadow) given to the head of each of the villages in the Five Great Countries is a symbol of their enormous power.

One of Naruto's first duties after becoming a Ninja is to protect and escort the bridge builder Tazuna back to his home country, the Land of Waves. This is a small country with no Ninja village and very little power to defend itself. Evil crime boss Gato is looking to take control of this country and it comes down to Naruto and his team to help stop him. This episode demonstrates how countries with no Ninja villages of their own are sometimes forced to seek the assistance of Ninja from other countries.

See Glossary
Konohagakure
Kirigakure
Sunagakure
Five Great Countries
Hokage
Kazekage
Otogakure
Gato

See questions
02 06

02 What's the relationship between the countries and their Shinobi villages?

It is said that the Shinobi villages were first founded when the Ninja clans moved out of the cities and built rural settlements in the mountains and countryside. Even during times of war, life in these villages was relatively stable on account of their military strength. Because of this, regular citizens began moving there too and they soon came to hold a status similar to that of independent countries (although they were still technically under the jurisdiction of countries they were founded in).

The feudal ruler of the country has the power to deploy these Shinobi villages in his land as a national defense force in the case of an attack or invasion from another country. In exchange, he provides them with financial aid and supplies. The head of the Shinobi village acts as the chief administrator for village affairs, while also being responsible for the defense of the country to which his village belongs. The power of the village, therefore, represents the military strength of the country. Because this relationship is what determines the power dynamic between the different countries, these villages are a necessity for the feudal lords. At the same time, for the villages to ensure a steady income and maintain their status, they must cooperate with the country they belong to. In effect the villages are on an equal footing with the countries they serve.

See questions
01 06

03 *What kind of work does a Ninja do?*

Historically, Ninja were hired as spies and assassins, paid by local feudal lords throughout Japan to gather information and eliminate rivals or informers. The Ninja of Naruto's world, however, are more like highly specialized soldiers who are trained to engage in all types of national military operations. At a local level they also perform the same kind of services as a general police force (including searching for lost pets!). They are a bit like local handymen, taking on work from a wide range of different people, including regular citizens and even citizens from other countries. There is a ranking system (A, B, C) by which the difficulty of each job is rated and the fee for the service calculated. The Ninja council decides this ranking and then decides what level of Ninja should be assigned to the task.

Before they can start working, Naruto and his classmates must first graduate from the Ninja Academy where they learn the basics of Ninjutsu. Once they pass the graduation exams, they are given the title of "Genin" (the lowest rank of

Ninja) and have their profile printed in the Ninja Yearbook. If they then get good marks in the selection exams they can go on to become mid-ranking Ninja or Chunin ("Journeyman" in the Viz translation). Those with even greater abilities become elite Ninja or Jonin. These high-ranking Ninja are entrusted with the most difficult tasks, as well as the instruction of lower ranking Ninja. The top Ninja of the village is usually appointed by the former Kage before he retires, but in cases where the former leader dies before naming a successor, the top Ninja of the village decide by council whom to nominate for the post.

The Ninja in Naruto's world are divided very strictly according to their level. Even if they are technically Ninja, if they don't keep moving up through the ranks, they will not be given full respect. Naruto's fixation on becoming "the next Lord Hokage" is based on his desire to be accepted and recognized by the people around him.

See Glossary
Ninja Academy
Genin
Chunin
Jonin
Hokage

See questions
08

04 So how does the Ninja society in Konohagakure work?

The Ninja of Konohagakure are divided into the following ranks according to their abilities: Lord Hokage, Tokubetsu (Special) Jonin, Jonin, Chunin and Genin. Just beneath the rank of Lord Hokage are the Ninja who form the Goikenban (Advisory Council). Below the Advisory Council are the various different military units such as the Seikibutai (Regular Military Unit), Iryohan (Medical Unit) and the Anbu ("Black Ops" – Viz). Each unit is commanded by a Tokubestu Jonin or Jonin who receives regular reports from their subordinates, and passes them up to Lord Hokage and the Advisory Council. Most Ninja belong to the Regular Military Unit, and trainee Ninja like Naruto and Sasuke start off being assigned there. The military units are further divided into teams or cells. The Medical Unit is split up into three smaller teams: a first-aid team which delivers medical aid on site during battles or tournaments; a team which works at the Konohagakure Hospital; and a research team which develops new medicines and healing techniques. Ninja are transferred from the Regular Military Unit to these kinds of specialist units according to their particular talents and abilities. Under the direct control of Lord Hokage is the Anbu unit, which carries out special assignments such as assassinations and internal surveillance – making sure that no enemy spies or informers are operating in the village. To ensure the integrity of its members, the Anbu unit always cover their faces with masks.

Some villages have other specialist units which don't exist in the Konohagakure system, such as the Oinin (Hunter-Nin) from Kirigakure. The Hunter-Nin are a special unit who assassinate Nukenin (Missing-Nin) – Ninja who have betrayed or left the village – and then dispose of the corpse. By analyzing the dead body of a Missing-Nin it is possible to learn many of the secret arts and techniques particular to village he or she is from. Because of this, the Hunter-Nin don't just assassinate their target, but also completely eradicate all traces of the body.

 ee Glossary

Genin
Chunin
Jonin
Hokage
Goikenban
Iryohan
Anbu
Uchiha Sasuke
Konohagakure
Kirigakure
Oinin
Nukenin

See questions
07

05 What's the story behind the Great Ninja Battle that took place before Naruto was born?

The Great Ninja Battle was a bitterly hard-fought war in which the Ninja villages scattered across the various lands all vied for supremacy with each other. As such it was not fought in the interests of the countries to which the Ninja villages belonged. During this period many great Ninja and new techniques emerged, but the huge numbers of casualties that came with it all but laid the countries to waste. To prevent this kind of battle ever re-occurring, the villages signed a treaty in which they agreed to supervize each other's military strength and to take care not to allow the fragile balance of power to fall apart again.

06 Does each village have its own set of Ninja techniques?

The kind of techniques a Ninja uses depends on the village they were brought up in. Sometimes this is determined by the natural features of the country the village is in. For example, in the desert-covered Land of Wind the Sunagakure Ninja are especially skilled at using sand in their techniques. The techniques developed by the original Kage of each village also play a role in shaping the particular style of Ninjutsu from that village. Konohagakure Ninja are masters of fire techniques, the Ninja from Sunagakure are skilled in the use of wind and Ninja from Kirigakure are able to use water to devastating effect. There is a definite tendency for the special skills of each village to mirror the elements in the village Kage's name (Lord Hokage: "Fire Shadow", Lord Kazekage: "Wind Shadow", Lord Mizukage: "Water Shadow"). At first glance it seems like the reason the leader of Konohagakure is called Lord Hokage (火影) is because the village is in the Land of Fire (火の国), but it is probably more accurate to say that the leaders of the villages chose their names to match their special skills.

The relationship between the names of the countries and villages is not explicitly talked about in the books, but it seems unlikely that a village leader with great skill in the use of fire techniques would coincidentally build a village in the Land of Fire, or that a leader skilled in water techniques would just happen to settle in the Land of Water. What is more likely is that the Five Great Countries were in fact named after the Kage that lived there. From the background information we are given, we know that the village of Konohagakure was founded 60 years prior to the beginning of the story. Of course the Land of Fire was around for a long time before that, but the world portrayed in the Naruto series is a world centered around Ninja – it is quite likely that the countries changed their names to fit their Ninja.

S ee Glossary

Sunakage
Konohagakure
Sunagakure
Kirigakure
Hokage
Kazekage
Five Great Countries

See questions
01 **02**

07 How do Ninja move up the "career ladder"?

The system varies from village to village, but if we take Konohagakure as an example, the first step on the road to Ninjahood begins with the Ninja Academy, where students fresh out of diapers start to learn the basics of Ninjustu. If they get a high enough mark in the Ninja Academy graduation exams the students can quit the academy and start their training as low-ranking Ninjas (Naruto fails this exam three times, but is able to graduate thanks to a little help from Iruka). Although Genin are given official status as Ninja they are still very much beginners. They are put into groups of three with their academy class-mates (Naruto was in class 3.1) and start to take on low level assignments under the guidance of a Jonin. These assignments make up the training required to progress to a higher class of Ninja. In many cases Genin fail to make the grade during training and have to go back to the academy (out of a group of 27 academy graduates, only nine make it as a Genin). In other words, even if you graduate from the Ninja Academy, it only means you have a shot at being a Genin and it doesn't mean that you have been accepted as a fully-fledged Ninja.

If the students successfully complete more than eight duties and the Jonin instructor judges that they have potential, then on the Jonin's recommendation, they can choose to take the Chunin exams. The villages of Konohagakure and Sunagakure hold their Chunin exams jointly. This is part of the treaty signed between the two countries intended to maintain the balance of power, but it is also a way of ensuring that only the highest quality of Ninja make it through this stage of their training. The standards for deciding who passes or fails this Chunin exam are vague. In fact, it depends entirely on the nomination of the judges. Unlike the academy graduation exams, a high mark is no guarantee of a pass. In the Chunin exams it is important to show the right attitude toward each task undertaken and to demonstrate that you can think like a real Ninja.

Becoming a Jonin is only possible through the recommendation of the other Jonin in the village. The system by which Ninja rise through the ranks in Konohagakure, therefore, depends largely on the recognition of the higher level Ninja above them.

See Glossary
Konohagakure
Ninja Academy
Ninjutsu
Genin
Chunin
Sunagakure

See questions
04

Naruto's Name is Right out of the Kitchen

The first thing that pops into a Japanese person's mind when they here the word "Naruto" is a kind of ramen topping made of steamed fish paste and decorated with a spiral pattern (incidentally, this pattern is called "uzumaki" in Japanese). Ramen almost always has a slice of naruto floating in it, making it a very familiar food to the ramen-loving Japanese people. It may seem odd to name your manga's hero after a kind of food, but Naruto creator Masashi Kishimoto has a history of getting his characters' names from the kitchen, starting from the manga he drew during childhood. Kishimoto has a twin brother, who also started drawing manga as a kid. His brother used insect names for his characters, but when he ran out of names, he had to look up new ones. On the other hand, when Masashi needed new names, he looked to the fridge, choosing names like Mayonnaise Man and Professor Pepper. So, his food-themed hero Uzumaki Naruto probably has a special place in Kishimoto's heart.

Other characters named after food include Anko (sweet bean paste), Inari (a kind of sushi), Udon (a variety of noodles) and Shimeji (shimeji mushroom).

08 What was the point of Naruto's first assignment as a Genin?

After Naruto, Sasuke and Sakura graduate from the academy, their first assignment is a "survival exercise". This is a tough test to see if Naruto and his teammates can forget about pursuing their own private goals and work together to complete the challenge. Instructor Kakashi attaches two bells to his waist. Whoever can steal one of these bells in the allotted time passes. Whoever fails to do so must return to the academy. This means that however hard they try, at least one of the three will come away empty-handed. As Kakashi predicts, Naruto and his teammates try their hardest to outdo each other in their attempts to get the bells. The real purpose of this exercise, however, is to test whether they are prepared to sacrifice their own glory for the good of the team. In the unwritten code of the Konohagakure Ninja, how you interact with your friends and teammates is considered more important than anything else. In a real-life situation, if you only think of yourself and act impulsively, you are not only putting your own life at risk, but also the lives of your teammates. During this exercise, Sasuke and Sakura share their lunch with Naruto, even though Kakashi has forbidden him any as a punishment. They do this is because they realize that a hungry Naruto is not going to be much use to the team. By doing this they pass the test. As Kakashi explains, helping your teammates is more important than obeying rules or commands. Through this exercise Kakashi teaches them to read "the hidden meanings within the hidden meanings". During training assignments the situation changes from moment to moment. Even if you are ordered not to do something, it sometimes becomes necessary to disobey the command in order to help your team or complete the task. This exercise is designed to test whether the three of them are flexible enough to adapt to each changing circumstance.

See Glossary

Uchiha Sasuke
Haruno Sakura
Hatake Kakashi
Konohagakure

See questions
03

In the Naruto series there many different types of Jutsu (techniques) used, but these can be broken down into three main groups.

Taijustu (Body Techniques) are the most basic form of Ninja techniques. The name refers to the kind of physical techniques (kicks and punches) used in martial arts such as Karate or Kung Fu. Taijutsu do not require the use of Chakra, so theoretically anyone can master them and, because they don't require any Hand Seals, they are the ideal form of attack in close-combat situations. In order to master Taijutsu, Ninja must train regularly to build up the muscles in their body. The one Taijustu which is the exception to the rule is Juken (Soft Technique), in which Chakra is used to inflict damage on the opponent's inner organs.

Ninjutsu (Ninja Techniques) require the Ninja to use his inner Chakra in order to perform various attack moves. Among the Ninja's arsenal of skills these techniques are some of the most important and spectacular to witness. First, the Ninja must collect the Chakra together in his body, turning spiritual energy in the body into a suitable form for the Ninjutsu that he or she is going to perform. The Ninja molds the Chakra, usually by forming a Hand Seal, and then lets fly with the Jutsu. How effective the Jutsu is depends on whether the Ninja can summon the right kind of Chakra for the technique, how much Chakra they can gather, and how quickly they can do it.

Genjutsu (Illusion Techniques) are mainly used to mess with an opponent's visual or audio sense – making them see or hear things that aren't there – but in some cases they are even used to control an opponent's mind. People who are especially skilled in this field are sometimes known as Genjutsushi.

In addition to these three main Jutsu there are also special Jutsu such as Juinjustu (Cursed Seal Techniques) which are used to control an opponent's spirit or body, Fuinjutsu (Sealing Techniques) which are used to seal something (eg. an evil spirit) inside a living being or object, and Hiden (Secret Arts) particular to a region or clan.

There are also some Ninjutsu whose effects are so terrible or the use of which are so dangerous that they are forbidden. These are known as Kinjutsu (Forbidden Arts).

Ⓢee Glossary

Taijutsu
Ninjutsu
Genjutsu
Rock Lee
Chunin exams
Chakra
Juinjutsu
Fuinjutsu
Hiden

See questions
10

10 So what exactly is Chakra?

Chakra is a word from the ancient Indian language of Sanskrit meaning "Circle" or "Wheel". It is what binds the body to the aura which surrounds the body. You could say it is like an "energy exchange" – a place where the aura is turned into physical energy. When this change is taking place, it works like a circular motion, which is why the word Chakra, meaning "Circle", is used.

In Naruto's world Chakra refers to the body and soul and comes from every one of the 130 trillion cells that are said to be in the body. When someone moves their arms or legs, or they think about someone they especially like, the physical and mental energy they are using is called "Stamina". The energy a Ninja takes from this stamina and uses in the execution of Ninjutsu is called Chakra. When performing Ninjutsu it is necessary to select and carefully compose the balance of the physical and mental energy and to match it to the Jutsu being performed. Because the composition of Chakra is different for each Jutsu, in order to master a Ninjutsu or Genjutsu technique the Ninja must also posses the ability to balance Chakra skillfully. As the Jutsu becomes more advanced, the amount of Chakra required becomes much greater and the balance of composition becomes even more intricate. If two different people perform the same Jutsu, whoever has less stamina will tire more quickly.

The amount of Chakra which is required to perform a particular technique is generally predetermined. If a Jutsu requires a Chakra level of 30 (for example), but the Ninja cannot channel that quantity, then they will be unable to perform the Jutsu properly. On the other hand, if they use a Chakra level of 40 or 50, then they will have wasted precious reserves and tired themselves out needlessly.

When Ninja perform a Jutsu (other than Taijutsu) they make a sign or seal with their fingers, which in turn molds and focuses the Chakra. The greater the degree of complexity of the Jutsu, the more difficult the seal is to make. Because of this, beginners attempting difficult Jutsu in the heat of battle sometimes leave themselves open to attack. How quickly a Ninja can compose seal in many ways determines that Ninja's level.

See Glossary
Chakra
Ninjutsu
Genjutsu
Rock Lee

See questions
09

11 *What is Kekkeigenkai?*

Kekkeigenkai is a term which denotes a special power or ability which is handed down through the generations of a Ninja clan via the bloodline. As such, these abilities are something that only members of a clan with that power can inherit. The Haku Clan is gifted with the Byakugan (White Eye) with which they are able to look inside a person's body and which gives them powers of clairvoyance and hypnosis. The Uchiha Clan posses the much desired Sharingan (Copy Wheel Eye) which allows them the ability to copy a Jutsu a split second after seeing it. However, because these clans possess these rare abilities, they are often ordered on dangerous missions or become the target of Ninja jealous of their special talents. As a result, there are only a few clans with Kekkeigenkai remaining. Being born to one of these clans doesn't necessarily mean you are gifted with that special ability, however, and even if you do inherit it, you don't know whether you have it or not until you begin to mature.

See Glossary

Kekkeigenkai
Byakugan
Sharingan
Haku
Hyuga Family

See questions
20 **33**

12 What are the Ningu that Ninja use?

The weapons and protective armor that Ninja use are known as Ningu (Ninja Tools). Typical examples of Ningu include Shuriken (throwing stars), Kunai (a kind of knife) and Makibishi (small spiked balls which are thrown on the ground to immobilize the enemy). Because a Ninja's degree of mobility is one of their most valuable assets they mainly use weapons that are light. Some Ninja also design their own original weapons (eg. Temari's giant fan).

Smoke bombs, Soldier Pills and other special medicines also share an important place in the Ninja's tool kit. The Soldier Pill is a kind of stimulant which allows the user to fight continuously for three days without taking a rest. Ninja who existed in Japan's past often used these kinds of drugs and were very knowledgeable about pharmaceutical science. Even today, pharmaceutical companies in Japan are often found clustered around areas, such as Toyama Prefecture, where there were formerly Ninja villages.

See Glossary
Ningu
Kunai
Makibishi

13 Naruto always carries a Makimono, but what is it for?

Makimono (Scrolls) in the Naruto series are used for four basic functions: reading, sealing, invoking a Jutsu, and making a contract. The most common of these four is reading – Ninja use the scrolls as a study aid to learn the Jutsu and seals, or as a reference tool (if they come across a technique during battle that they haven't seen before they can later learn what it is called and decipher what kind of system it is). In Uzumaki Naruto's case, he uses his scrolls almost exclusively as a crib sheet, because he is always forgetting how to do techniques. This explains why he usually carries one around with him.

Using scrolls to "seal" something (commonly a spirit of some type) is a special technique called Fuinjutsu (Seal Techniques) and requires a great degree of skill. The Fuinjustu itself is a predetermined set of characters and ideograms which, when written on a blank scroll, have the power to trap and seal whatever it is the Ninja is trying to capture (like the seal on Naruto's stomach which keeps the Nine-Tailed Fox Spirit imprisoned). Ninja who are especially skilled at Fuinjutsu always carry a blank scroll around with them just in case.

There are also special, pre-written scrolls that can be used to perform Jutsu just by opening them up. For example, if a Ninja unrolls a scroll with a hypnosis technique written inside, they can hypnotize their opponent as effectively as someone skilled in hypnotic arts, even if they have never learnt how to do the technique themselves.

The final important role Makimono play is in creating the contract required for Kuchiyose (Summoning Techniques). A Kuchiyose technique is one in which a Ninja can call an animal to his or her aid during battle. In Jiraiya's case this is a giant frog, in Tsunade's a huge slug. In order to be able to do this kind of technique, it is necessary to have signed a contract with the animal in question. As proof of the contract both the Ninja and animal's names are written on the scroll – sometimes in blood. Even if a Ninja performs a Kuchiyose technique, without this contract nothing will come to their aid.

See Glossary
Fuinjutsu
Kuchiyose

The NARUTO SAGA

part02

Naruto & his friends' Secrets

14 | *So what's the story with the Nine-tailed Fox Spirit?*

Before the serialization of Naruto, author Masashi Kishimoto published "Naruto" as a one-shot manga. In this shortened version, Naruto was presented as the child of the Nine-Tailed Fox Spirit. When the serialization in Shonen Jump began it seemed that Naruto was actually the reincarnation of the Nine-Tailed Fox Spirit and that this was the reason why the people of the village loathed and despised him. However as the series progressed, it became clear that Naruto is in fact a normal human being.

In a dramatic episode that takes place before the beginning of the story, the fourth Lord Hokage confronts a terrifyingly powerful Fox Spirit which is attempting to destroy the village of Konohagakure. To bring an end to the ordeal he performs a Fuinjutsu (Sealing Technique), imprisoning the spirit in the newly-born Naruto and sacrificing his own life in the process. Naruto is therefore physically a normal human being, but because he has the Fox Spirit inside his body, the villagers fear that at some point it will take control of his spirit and wreak destruction on the village once more. If that were to happen you really could say that Naruto was being reincarnated as the Nine-Tail Fox Spirit. It seems kind of unfair though, that the villagers treat him so harshly. By carrying this evil spirit inside him, Naruto has done the village a great service – really they should be thanking him.

As the story progresses, we can see that the villagers' fears are not completely unfounded. At certain key moments Naruto suddenly bursts forth with overwhelming power and it is obvious that his Chakra is getting a boost from the Fox Spirit. At these times it is not always clear who's in control. What is clear is that the Fox Spirit is still very much alive and well and the possibility that it will take over Naruto's spirit one day can definitely not be ruled out…

See Glossary
Nine-Tailed Fox Spirit
Konohagakure
Chakra

15 | Who are Naruto's parents?

Because Naruto is a normal human being we know that he must have had parents, but in the manga series nothing is said about them explicitly. Among Naruto fans in Japan, there is a generally accepted theory that Naruto is actually the son of the fourth Lord Hokage. Whenever there is any mention of him, the fourth Lord Hokage is portrayed as a deeply caring figure with a strong sense of justice. The idea is that, even during the encounter with the Fox Spirit when the village was in its darkest hour, there is no way this Lord Hokage would allow anyone else's child but his own to be sacrificed. Most likely it was the very fact of Naruto's birth that gave him the opportunity to deal with the Fox Spirit in this way. There is not a lot of information about the fourth Lord Hokage (as of volume 27 of the Japanese manga his name is still unknown), but when you consider how young he was when he became Lord Hokage it seems possible that he might have been the son of the original or second Lord Hokage. Something that we learn later in the story is that the first and second Lord Hokage were brothers. If the fourth Lord Hokage were one of their sons, and if Naruto is his son, then it follows that Naruto is in fact a direct descendent of the Hokage bloodline.

From the very beginning of the series Naruto is always talking about his dream to become Lord Hokage – not just a high-raking Ninja, but Lord Hokage himself. Perhaps author Masashi Kishimoto wants us to read the "hidden meaning within the hidden meaning", that this is because Naruto is of the same blood.

See Glossary
Hokage

See questions
18

16 Why is Naruto so good at the Kagebunshin technique?

For the first ten volumes of the series the Kagebunshin technique (Shadow Clone Jutsu, or "Art of the Doppelganger" – Viz) is Naruto's most advanced skill and he often uses it when the going gets tough. Naruto's Kagebunshin is special in that each incarnation of himself that he conjures is actual flesh and blood and operates with its own will (normally Ninja performing this technique are only able to create an image of their body). This technique is usually used to throw the enemy into confusion, but in Naruto's case he can also use it to attack the enemy from several different directions at once. Ordinarily there is no way Naruto could master a technique that even Jonin consider advanced. In fact, Ninjutsu is not Naruto's strong point in general. So feeling that he needs some new skills quick and not wanting to spend years of training acquiring them, Naruto decides to take a short cut and steals a secret manuscript from the third Lord Hokage's house. This scroll contains instructions on all the most advanced techniques that have been developed in the village of Konohagakure over the generations. Among these is the Kagebunshin technique.

While this technique is recorded in the secret manuscript it is actually a Kinjutsu (Forbidden Art), so is potentially very dangerous to use. It requires a huge amount of Chakra and lower-ranking Ninja are not usually able perform it. Naruto is certainly not a master of Chakra-control, but he does have an extra source of Chakra inside him, thanks to the Fox Spirit. It is this which allows him to perform this unusual skill.

So why is it dangerous? Well, when Naruto performs this technique, each clone he creates is real and can act independently of the original body. This means that it is possible to attack an opponent from all sides (in Naruto's case he can conjure up hundreds of clones), but if that opponent then uses a Genjutsu technique then you've got a lot of confused clones! When the clones start to lose the plot, then they can end up fighting with each other and even, in the worst case scenario, killing the Ninja performing the technique. In fact, in several fights Naruto does actually get hit by his own doppelganger.

See Glossary

Kagebunshin
Konohagakure
Ninjutsu
Kinjutsu
Genjutsu

While he is at the academy, Naruto's weakest technique is the Art of Transformation (Henge). Whenever he tries to change into something, he always ends up changing into something completely different. The only thing that Naruto is really good at transforming into is a beautiful, naked girl. He calls this the Oiroke no Jutsu ("Ninja Centerfold" –Viz). While guys go crazy over it, it's not altogether clear how useful this skill is. But why is it that Naruto, who is usually so bad at transformation techniques, can turn himself into a beautiful, naked girl at will?

From ancient times the fox has had a mythical status in Japan – legend has it that fox spirits have the ability to change themselves into the female form. There are stories of how a fox would change its form to a beautiful woman in order to put a Samurai off his guard and then steal his wallet. Even today if a woman commits some act of fraud, Japanese people will often refer to them as Megitsune (女狐), which translates literally as "fox woman". Naruto is a master of the Ninja

Centerfold because he has a fox spirit inside him. He sometimes uses the fox's power without even realizing it.

Historically female Ninja in Japan were known as Kunoichi and they very often used their sexual charm as a weapon to put their male opponents off guard. Even though he is a guy, by performing the Ninja Centerfold, Naruto can also use this kind of tactic. Maybe it is a handy trick after all…it certainly seems to work on Lord Hokage…

S ee Glossary
Oiroke no Jutsu
Hokage

The popularity of the name "Sasuke" in Ninja manga

Sasuke is Naruto's friend and rival. Actually, this name is very commonly given to Ninja in Japanese fiction, and many Japanese probably mentally connect the name Sasuke with Ninjutsu. The roots of this go back to a series of novels titled "Sarutobi Sasuke" that were written in the Taisho era (1912-1926). Sasuke is a fictional Ninja, but in the novels he appears as one of the ten heroes of Sanada Yukimura, an actual warlord during the Warring States period. The novels were a huge hit, and the name Sasuke became associated with Ninja characters. This association was further cemented in the 60s when Sanpei Shirato created a manga about a young Ninja named Sasuke. This manga also enjoyed great popularity, and was turned into a television anime series. In modern times, the manga Sasuke probably had more to do with popularizing this name as a conventional Ninja name.

Going back to the novel, Sasuke's family name Sarutobi has also become associated with Ninja. This connection can be seen in the character Sarutobi (the third Lord Hokage) and in Asuma Sarutobi's name.

18 Is there any chance that Naruto will become Lord Hokage?

When the first Lord Hokage died his younger brother acceded to the position as the second Lord Hokage. Sarutobi, who was formerly a pupil of the first and second Lord Hokage, was then the third person to take the job. The fourth Lord Hokage was a former a pupil of Jiraiya, who was himself one of Sarutobi's pupils, making the fourth Lord Hokage a "grand-disciple" of Sarutobi. The fourth Lord Hokage then dies at an early age (saving the village from the nine-tailed fox spirit), after which the third Lord Hokage accedes to the position for a second time. When the third Lord Hokage dies in a fight against Orochimaru, his pupil Tsunade becomes the fifth Lord Hokage. The decision of who becomes the next Lord Hokage is made by the Jonin in the village, but it is clear that there are strong ties linking each Lord Hokage with one or more of their predecessors. Some fans speculate for this reason that the fourth Lord Hokage is the son of the first or second Lord Hokage. In any case, blood-ties and master-pupil relationships definitely seem to play a large part in deciding who gets the job.

Tsunade (the fifth Lord Hokage) looks young but is in her fifties so is unlikely to carry on for much longer in the position. Currently the strongest candidate for a successor is the pupil of the fourth Lord Hokage, Hatake Kakashi. If Kakashi were to succeed as the sixth Lord Hokage then the chances of one of his pupils (Naruto, Sasuke or Sakura) becoming his successor are very high. Naruto begins to looks like a particularly strong candidate in volume 11 when Jiraiya (the pupil of the third Lord Hokage) starts to train him in Ninjutsu. It may even be that Jiraiya takes over Naruto's tutelage with this goal in mind. For this reason alone, Naruto seems the most likely out of his team to become the future Lord Hokage. But if we then accept the fans' theory that Naruto is the son of the fourth Lord Hokage, then his chances seem even greater.

See Glossary

Hokage
Jiraiya
Orochimaru
Tsunade
Hatake Kakashi
Uchiha Sasuke
Haruno Sakura

See questions
15

19 Is the Rasengan technique that Jiraiya teaches Naruto really that great?

Naruto's Rasengan (Spiraling Sphere) technique is still in its early stages and he has not yet perfected it. It is a technique that the fourth Lord Hokage took three years to master so is a very difficult and very advanced technique. To perform it you must focus all the Chakra energy you can summon into the palm of your hand and then compress it by whizzing it around violently. You then fire this spherical mass of Chakra at your opponent. This ball is only the size of a fist, but it has the destructive force of a hurricane. Once perfected it is said that there is no known defense against it. The best thing about this technique is that there is no need to make a finger seal to do it. This means you don't leave yourself open to attack.

The drawback is that this technique requires a lot of Chakra. The Rasengan suits Naruto well, because he has good stamina so can summon quite a lot of Chakra and he can also draw on the Chakra of the Nine-Tailed Fox Spirit inside him.

The fact that this technique doesn't require tricky finger seals is an added bonus for Naruto (seals are not his strongest point). For the time being, however, in order for Naruto to perform this technique he must first perform the Art of the Doppelganger and use his clones' hands to help him make the ball. The problem is that to perform the Art of the Doppelganger he has to use a certain amount of Chakra, which means he can't devote all of his power to the Rasengan. Well, it's a work in progress...

See Glossary

Rasengan
Nine-Tailed Fox Spirit

20 How high-ranking is the Uchiha Clan?

The Uchiha Clan was formerly the highest ranking clan in the village of Konohagakure. For generations the Uchiha Clan had been entrusted with the job of running the Konohagakure Police Force and they were respected throughout the village. Sasuke's father, Fugaku, and elder brother, Itachi, were both great Ninja. Even though Sasuke always got top marks while he was at the Ninja Academy, he feels a great pressure to live up to his family's name. The secret to the power of this Clan is the Sharingan – a Kekkeigenkai ability passed down the blood-line. For a Ninja, possessing an eye which allows them to see through their opponents thoughts or read their techniques puts them at a great advantage.

In addition to the Sharingan, the basic level of skill of the Uchiha Clan is also very high and they have produced many outstanding Ninja over the years. Sasuke himself is generally considered to show big potential. When Kakashi teaches him the Chidori (Thousand Birds) technique, Sasuke masters it in almost no time at all. Even without the Sharingan, Sasuke would still be one of the best Ninja in his year.

See Glossary

Uchiha Clan
Konohagakure Police
Uchiha Fugaku
Uchiha Itachi
Sharingan
Kekkeigenkai
Hatake Kakashi
Chidori

See questions
11

47

21 Do Sasuke and Naruto really not get along?

When Sasuke was very young the whole of his clan was wiped out by his elder brother Itachi. This must have been an incredibly traumatic event for Sasuke, who looked up his brother more than anyone else. Since then, taking revenge on Itachi has basically been his sole reason for living. As well as suffering the pain of losing his family, Sasuke must have had a very lonely childhood and he surely feels some sympathy with Naruto, who also lost his family at an early age. He often comes across as cold and distant, but deep down inside Sasuke definitely feels a great deal of friendship towards Naruto, even if he doesn't always show it.

Naruto feels a sense of rivalry towards Sasuke, but this is mainly because of his crush on Sakura (who only has eyes for Sasuke). For Naruto, nothing is more important than the people he cares about and he clearly cares a lot about Sasuke.

However, as time goes on, more and more obstacles stand in the way of their friendship. Sasuke believes that his brother Itachi is the most powerful Ninja alive, so in order to take his revenge on him, he himself must become the greatest Ninja of all. By contrast, Naruto's goal in life is to become the future Lord Hokage and win the recognition of the village. The more skills and strength Naruto acquires in this quest, the more of a threat he becomes to Sasuke's ambitions of being the greatest living Ninja. As the story progresses we begin to sense that Sasuke's heart is gradually hardening towards his old teammate. While Naruto tends to think of his friends as people who must be protected, Sasuke sees other people only in terms of how their skills and powers compare to his. Perhaps he finds Naruto's overbearing sense of camaraderie a little tiresome.

When Itachi returns to the village on some errand, Sasuke tries to exact his revenge. However, the Chidori (Thousand Birds) technique he has been working on doesn't even scratch him. What really gets to Sasuke, though, is the interest his brother takes in Naruto. Not only does Sasuke realize how far he has to go to match brother's skill, Itachi doesn't even give him the time of day. From that point on Sasuke begins to despise Naruto. The story is still in progress so we don't know what the eventual outcome of Naruto and Sasuke's relationship will be, but it would be nice to think that they end up being friends again.

See Glossary
Uchiha Sasuke
Hokage
Uchiha Itachi
Chidori

See questions
23

22 Will Sasuke abandon the village of Konohagakure?

Having re-met his brother but been unable to take his revenge, Sasuke decides to become stronger by whatever means he can and goes to seek the help of the evil Orochimaru. Orochimaru first appears in the story during the Chunin exams, which he uses as an opportunity to stage a coup d'etat against the village. He fails to take the village, but implants a Juin (Cursed Seal) in Sasuke's neck so that he will later come to see him of his own accord. Orochimaru does this because he needs Sasuke's body in order to continue living (and because he wants the Sharingan). Those who fall prey to Orochimaru's Juinjutsu gain awesome amounts of power, but pay for it with their soul. However Sasuke has reached a point where he will stop at nothing to become powerful, even if it means becoming Orochimaru's puppet.

When Naruto realizes that Sasuke has left the village to go in search of Orochimaru, he tries desperately to stop him, but the Juin in his neck has given Sasuke new-found strength, and he beats Naruto in a final showdown.

See Glossary
Orochimaru
Juinjutsu
Sharingan

23 Why did Sasuke's brother Itachi kill all the members of his clan?

I
tachi was a member of the Konohagakure's highest-ranking clan and, among them, was considered to be the most highly-skilled Ninja. At the age of seven he graduated top of his year from the Ninja Academy, at eight he developed the Shashingan (Photographic Eye), and at thirteen he was made the head of an Anbu unit. His father had great expectations of him and from a very young age his talents were encouraged to bloom. With his credentials he could have even become a future Lord Hokage. How did he end up going so far off the rails as to try and wipe out his own family..? It can only have been because he was *too* good. The Uchiha always put the prosperity and welfare of the clan before anything else. Itachi, it seems, could no longer stand the feeling of being held back by his family, so decided to remove them from the equation – a classic tale of genius turned to madness. Having left the village in search of freedom and new possibilities, Itachi now belongs to a group called Akatsuki (Dawn). Why someone who had gone so far to be liberated

from his "family bonds" should then go and join another kind of group is never really explained.

See Glossary

Uchiha Itachi
Konohagakure
Ninja Academy
Akatsuki

See questions
21

A t the beginning of the series, it seems that Sakura only wants to be a Ninja so she can be together with her beloved Sasuke. She certainly never shows the determination to succeed as a Ninja that her two teammates do. From an early age Sakura was shy and bullied and her classmate Ino was the only person who was ever kind to her. Of the two, Ino always seemed like the more talented Ninja, but during the Chunin exams she competes against Sakura and loses (but only just).

Sakura excels at school work and although she's not really into fighting, she is the best of the three in her team at controlling Chakra. When the fifth Lord Hokage, Tsunade, discovers Sakura's skill at performing medical techniques, she is able to tap the true potential of her talent. Medical care is a field which is ideally suited to Ninja like Sakura, who have book smarts and can control their Chakra well. Like Tsunade, it turns out that Sakura has actually been hoarding huge amounts of power.

The second cycle of the Naruto saga is currently being serialized in Japan (this book deals with the first cycle, up to vol 27). There are likely to be more and more scenes focusing on Sakura in the forthcoming volumes. As author Masashi Kishimoto probably intends the reader to notice, the qualities represented in Naruto, Sasuke and Sakura very closely resemble those of the Legendary Three Ninja, Jiraiya, Orochimaru and Tsunade. Jiraiya is a big-hearted, humorous character with slightly lecherous tendencies in whom we can definitely see something of a Naruto-of-the-future (Jiraiya's unrequited love for Tsunade also has a faint echo of Naruto's longing for Sakura, although at this stage Naruto's feelings are not much more than a schoolboy crush). Sasuke and Orochimaru both have the same kind of dark nature, prodigious talents and desire to do whatever it takes to become powerful. Tsunade and Sakura share a talent for medical techniques, as well as a great ability for controlling Chakra. Naruto, Sasuke and Sakura; maybe one day they will also be known as the Legendary Three Ninja...

⑤ee Glossary

Haruno Sakura
Chunin exams
Chakra
Tsunade
Uchiha Sasuke
Orochimaru
Jiraiya
Legendary Three Ninja

Naruto's teacher Kakashi is a highly accomplished Ninja with more than a fighting chance at becoming the next Lord Hokage after Tsunade. His secret strength is his Sharingan (Copy Eye Wheel). The Sharingan is a Kekkeigenkai power of the Uchiha Clan and would normally only be passed on to members of the clan with that DNA. Kakashi's Sharingan, however, is not originally his own eye.

In his younger days Kakashi was part of a team of three along with Obito and Rin. These were the dark days of the Great Ninja Battle when "duties" meant going into combat. Kakashi's father, Hatake Sakumo (aka "White Fang") was an outstanding Ninja, but during an assignment one of his team-mates was taken captive and he was forced to choose between carrying on with the mission and rescuing his colleague. He chose to rescue his friend and abandoned the mission, for which the other Ninja in the village severely criticized him. The story ended in Sakumo's tragic suicide.

Having seen what happened to his father, Kakashi grew up a cool-headed Ninja who valued completing the mission above everything else. During one assignment, his teammate Rin is taken captive and Kakashi abandons her in order to complete the mission. Obito criticizes him for this, telling him that while those who don't follow the rules and code of the Ninja are worthless, those who don't look out for their teammates are even worse. He goes off to rescue Rin on his own and Kakashi runs after him, but is unable to prevent his Obito's heroic death. As proof of his friendship, in his dying moments Obito gives one of his eyes to Kakashi, who has just lost one of his own in a previous fight. Obito was a member of the Uchiha Clan and his eye houses the much-coveted Sharingan.

It is this episode that makes Kakashi aware of the true nature of friendship. The very first thing he teaches Naruto and his team is the importance of valuing your teammates. The words he uses are the same words his friend Obito says to him shortly before he dies.

See Glossary
Hatake Kakashi
Hokage
Tsunade
Uchiha Obito
Rin
Hakake Sakumo

26 Why is Kakashi called the "Copy" Ninja?

With the Sharingan comes a special skill called the Jutsuutsushi (lit. Technique Copy). This skill allows the user in a split-second to read and analyze whatever technique his opponent is performing, even when it's a Jutsu he or she has never encountered before. If you can understand the mechanism behind a technique you can use it for yourself. (Of course, if you don't have enough skill to perform the Jutsu in the first place, the Sharingan does not help much). Kakashi is called the "Copy" Ninja, because he has enough skill and ability to analyze almost any kind of technique his opponent might use, and, within an instant, use it himself. Combined with his speed, dexterity and strength, this ability to copy his enemy's moves makes Kakashi a formidable sparring partner.

See Glossary
Hatake Kakashi
Sharingan

27 Is it true that Kakashi was voted no. 1 in a readers' poll?

In Shonen Jump (the weekly magazine in which Naruto is serialized in Japan) there are regular readers' polls to see which characters are the most popular. In the very first poll held, surprisingly it was not the hero of the story, Naruto, who came first, but Kakashi! Although Naruto stole first place in the next poll, Kakashi has won on many other occasions since then and he and Naruto effectively share the top spot. Even though there aren't very many episodes which focus specifically on him in the serialized manga, Kakashi is popular with men and women readers alike and is often cited as the "ideal boss". Kakashi is definitely one of the most interesting characters – his passion for romantic (or sexy?) novels, disheveled appearance and laid-back character has won the hearts of fans not just in Japan, but the world over.

See Glossary
Hatake Kakashi

Iruka is a teacher at the Konohagakure Ninja Academy, whose kindness and passion for teaching earns him the trust of all the children he encounters. Now 24, he first became a Chunin at the age of 16. Given the pressure on Ninja in the Konohagakure system to keep progressing up the ranks, it would be fair to assume that he has remained a Chunin because of his lack of talent. However, Iruka's talents lie elsewhere. Under normal circumstances Iruka is expected to carry out his regular duties in addition to teaching the students at the Academy. After Orochimaru's attempted coup d'etat the Konohagakure is in a state of turmoil and there is much work to do to restore order. Even at this busy time, though, Iruka makes sure to watch over each and every student and give them his support and affection. Part of Iruka's passion for teaching is born out of the loss of his parents to the Nine-Tailed Fox Spirit and the lonely youth he experienced as a result. He was also present when the Fox Spirit was finally defeated, so witnessed the fourth Lord Hokage's heroic sacrifice to protect the village. These two major events both helped shape Iruka's spirit of compassion – a spirit which resonates with the values instilled in the village since its foundation (the first Lord Hokage gave the name "Hi no Ishi", which literally translates as "Fire Mind", to the concept of protecting the village).

Iruka, therefore, has all the right qualifications to teach at the Konohagakure Ninja Academy. He is also the first person Naruto is really able to open up his heart to and comes to be something of a father figure to him. He may not be the most powerful Ninja, but he is certainly a pillar of village life.

S ee Glossary

Umino Iruka
Ninja Academy
Chunin
Orochimaru
Nine-Tailed Fox Sprit

S urprisingly, only one person passes the Chunin selection exams: Nara Shikamaru. It is particularly ironic that of all the A-grade Genin who take the exam Shikamaru, who shows almost no ambition, should be selected. He doesn't seem to be especially strong or skilled, and while his Kagemane (Shadow Imitation) technique is well-honed, it is not exactly what you'd call devastating...

However, the fact that he got chosen to become a Chunin demonstrates what the Ninja of Konohagakure consider the most important criteria for selection. What sets Shikamaru apart from the other Genin during the exam is his ability to assesses his surroundings and then to act in the most effective way. Whatever situation Shikamaru finds himself in, he is always thinking one or two moves ahead. He doesn't try and confront the situation head on, and prefers to go with the flow, allocating the other members of his team to different roles according to their individual abilities. This skill of making the best of whatever resources are available to him is what makes him such a good leader.

In other words, as far as the Chunin exam judges are concerned, the most important thing of all is "Team Work" and the people with the qualities to be a team leader are prized above everyone else. In the fight with Temari, Shikamaru really comes into his own as a tactician. Although he eventually concedes defeat, he is constantly appraising the situation and employing the right response. Even his decision to give up is the best move for Shikamaru who realizes he can't win and doesn't want to be killed just for the sake of his pride. In the end it proves a smart move – though he never does anything really spectacular during the Chunin exams, he clearly catches the eye of the judges with his tactical abilities.

S **ee Glossary**
Chunin exams
Nara Shikamaru
Genin
Kagemane

kimichi Choji is always eating and some might say he is…well…fat. Those who do say so to his face, soon regret it. For Choji it is the ultimate insult, and if anyone calls him that he goes crazy and unleashes his full power on them. But if he hates being called fat so much then why doesn't he go on a diet? The reason is that Choji's power actually lies in his excessive eating. One of Konohagakure's highest ranking families, the Akimichi Clan have for generations specialized in making Hiyaku (Secret Medicine), and particularly medicines which are taken orally. Among these are special pills which have the effect of reinvigorating Chakra – in other words, members of Akimichi Clan use the act of eating as a form of attack.

The most secret of the Secret Medicines that the Akimichi Clan specializes in is the Sanshoku no Ganyaku (Three Colored Pills). These are red, blue and yellow pills that contain vast amounts of energy and if you swallow one you get an enormous boost in power. However this is sometimes accompanied by some very bad side effects. With blue the weakest and red the strongest, as the strength of the pills increases, so to does the severity of the side effects. The red pill is so powerful that it can sometimes even result in death. Choji uses these pills to help him perform the Baika no Jutsu (a technique where his body more than doubles in size), which he combines with other Jutsu such as the Nikudansensha (Meat Tank).

See Glossary

Akimichi Choji
Sanshoku no Ganyaku
Akimichi Clan
Baika no Jutsu
Nikudansensha

31 | How unusual are the bug techniques that Aburame Shino uses?

Ninjustu that involves the use of bugs is a specialty of the Aburame Clan. There don't seem to be any other Ninja who use bugs in their techniques, so you could say it was a pretty unique talent. While it is fairly common for Ninja to summon animals to fight with them using Kuchiyose techniques, in Shino's case he gathers bugs at home, deliberately encourages parasites to live in his body and then learns to control them. In this way, without even invoking a Kuchiyose technique, he can deploy them in battle. By using these bugs he can perform the Bunshin (Clone) technique to create his own bug-doppelganger. He can also attach the scent of a female moth to his opponent and then have him pursued by swarms of male moths. If he gets poisoned, he puts bugs which eat the poisonous agents into his body and they will eat them.

Shino's ingenious techniques make excellent use of the bugs' natural habits – the result, perhaps, of years of research by his clan into bug behavior.

See Glossary

Aburame Shino
Ninjutsu
Aburame Clan
Kuchiyose

32 Why does Inzuka Kiba usually carry a dog around with him?

Members of Kiba's Inuzuka Clan have always worked together with dogs which are known as Ninken (Ninja Dog). Kiba's Ninken is called Akamaru, and they are an inseparable team, always at each other's side. Akamaru is also different to the animals usually summoned using the Kuchiyose technique. Because he is always with Kiba, Akamaru is almost like an extension of Kiba's body. Having trained together from an early age, he is highly skilled at Ninjutsu techniques which he performs in combination with his master.

The Inuzuka Clan themselves have very sensitive noses. They like to use their fangs and claws during battle and train in order to acquire the same kind of skills as wild animals. This is called Giju Ninpo (lit. Beast Imitation Ninja Technique). Kiba has mastered a variation of Giju Ninpo called Gijin Ninpo (where he turns Akamaru into a human being), and which he also combines with a cloning technique called Jujin Bunshin (Half-Beast Clone). Because he carries out the Jujin

Bushin technique in combination with Akamaru, it can be performed without using much Chakra, while still creating the same effect as a regular cloning technique. Kiba's most advanced move is probably the Gatsuga technique (lit. Double Fang Wolf) where he partners with Akamaru and, in a kind of half-wolf state, flies towards his opponent spinning at dizzying speed.

These highly-technical combination moves are only possible because Kiba and Akamaru constantly train together. Akamaru is not just Kiba's cute little pet, but an integral part of his whole Ninja style.

S ee Glossary

Inuzuka Kiba
Ninken
Kuchiyose
Akamaru
Chakura
Gatsuga

Neji was born from the noble Hyuga Clan (a Kekkeigenkai family) in the village of Konohagakure. He has been blessed with special power of that clan perhaps more than any other member. But while Neji clearly thinks he is pretty hot stuff as a Ninja, he feels a sense of inferiority because he is born from a side branch of the Hyuga family. Hinata, on the other hand, is a descendent of the main branch of the family. Within the clan there is a rule that states that if the main branch of the family is ever in need of protection, then the side branches must sacrifice themselves. Neji and Hinata's fathers were born into this world as twins. Hinata's father Hiashi later became the head of the clan. However, because Neji's father was born second and was therefore the younger brother, he was demoted to a side branch of the family. During an episode in which the Hyuga Clan came under threat, in order to protect Hiashi from assassination, Neji's father stepped in as his body double and was killed as a result. Wracked by grief at his father's death, Neji cursed fate for the cruel hand it had dealt him – if his father had just been born before Hiashi, he would have been the head of the clan and Neji would have been a member of the main family… However much he trains to be a Ninja, and however skilled he becomes, he can never change the fate that has been handed him by the Hyuga Clan… That pent-up anger and resentment finds expression in the rage with which he attacks Hinata, who is herself not especially skilled as a Ninja and whose only distinction is that she is a member of the main family. This is a distinction, in fact, which Hinata could happily do without. All her life she has been pressured to become a Ninja and represent the Hyuga Clan, even though it is clear she has no special Ninja talents.

Through his dealings with Naruto, Neji begins to change his outlook on life. He realizes that fate does not have to decide everything, and that it is possible to control your own destiny. Once he learns this, his attitude towards Hinata must also surely change.

S ee Glossary

Hyuga Neji
Hyuga Clan
Kekkeigenkai
Konohagakure
Hyuga Hinata
Hyuga Hiashi

See questions
11

34 Can hard-working Rock Lee ever become a top-ranking Ninja?

Not just anyone can become a Jonin – the kind of talents you are born with determine to a large extent the level you can reach as a Ninja. If you consider that the well-established clans from Konohagakure (Uchiha, Hyuga, Akimichi, Inuzuka etc) have all produced outstanding Ninja through the generations, you can see that skill is closely related to the genes that run in the family.

Rock Lee is not descended from any of those clans and as a result lacks the Chakra necessary to perform Ninjustu and Genjutsu. He can only use Taijutsu techniques. Under the tutelage of Might Guy, however, Lee has honed these techniques to an extraordinary level just through hard work and pure determination.

It is obvious that deep down Rock Lee knows that he is not a great Ninja, but he can never allow himself to give up. His strength is in his ability to set his sights high and to strive to achieve his goals, convincing himself all the while that one day he really will become a top-level Jonin.

Author Masashi Kishimoto almost certainly named Rock Lee as a nod to the late Bruce Lee (they even have the same hairstyle). Like Rock Lee, Bruce Lee was all about Taijutsu techniques and never included anything like the Genjutsu or Ninjutsu that appear in the Naruto series in any of his movies. While there is no question that Bruce Lee was master of martial arts, he probably wouldn't stand a chance against most of the Konohagakure Ninja. For the same reason it seems unlikely that Rock Lee will ever achieve his goal of being a high-level Ninja.

Ⓢee Glossary
Rock Lee
Uchiha Clan
Hyuga Clan
Akimichi Clan
Chakra
Ninjutsu
Genjutsu
Taijutsu
Might Guy

See questions
35 **39**

Might Guy is a Jonin and contemporary of Hatake Kakashi. While Kakashi's father was a great Ninja who went by the name of White Fang, Might Guy was not born into a legendary Ninja clan and came from a more humble background. As a result he has always considered Kakashi as a rival, and in his youth constantly strived to surpass his skills. Through sheer determination to match Kakashi, Guy was eventually able to become a Jonin level Ninja. Because of his past, Guy sees something of himself in the young Rock Lee, and cherishes him like a son.

Unlike Lee, though, Guy is not just limited to using Taijutsu. While not particularly skilled at them, he can also perform some Genjutsu techniques. If you look at his career record, you can see he graduated from the Ninja Academy aged seven, and was selected as a Chunin at the age of eleven, which suggests that he was born with some natural talent. Guy's appearances in the story are generally in connection with Lee, so it is easy to assume that he too can only perform Taijustu techniques, but this is not the case.

See Glossary
Rock Lee
Uchiha Clan
Hyuga Clan
Akimichi Clan
Chakra
Ninjutsu
Genjutsu
Taijutsu
Might Guy

See questions
34

36 Why is the third Lord Hokage also known as the "Professor"?

The first Lord Hokage who founded the village of Konohagakure invented the original Ninjutsu technique of Mokuton Hijutsu (lit. Wood Release Secret Art). His younger brother the second Lord Hokage then developed this technique further.

The third Lord Hokage was a pupil of both the first and second Lord Hokage. He not only mastered the Mokuton Hijustsu, but all the techniques that were developed in the village of Konohagakure. An ardent researcher of Ninjutsu, he has whole library of scrolls at his house filled with different techniques. His depth of knowledge about Ninjutsu at some point earned him the nickname of "Professor". While the word "professor" has certain scholarly associations, the third Lord Hokage is definitely not an aloof, academic type. He treats all the Ninja in the village as though they were his own children and he is loved and respected by everyone. He was also the mentor of the Legendary Three Ninja, which suggests that he must have been a very good teacher.

See Glossary
Hokage
Professor
Ninjutsu
Legendary Three Ninja

E bisu is the home tutor of Konohamaru, the grandchild of the third Lord Hokage. A lot of readers may assume that his main profession is private teaching, but he is in fact a Tokubetsu (Special) Jonin with very respectable Ninja credentials. He likes to claim that he has trained numerous candidates for the position of Lord Hokage. We learn later, however, that the system for being nominated as a Lord Hokage depends on the recommendation of several Jonin and the length of the term in the position is not fixed. Given these factors it seems that Ebisu's claim is a bit of an empty boast (can you really be considered a "candidate" for a position when it might not become vacant for another 20 years..?)

That aside, the question here is, how much does Ebisu really teach Konomaru? There are times when it's clear that the relationship between Ebisu and Konohamaru is really not very good. Until he meets Naruto, Konomaru has issues with his status as grandson to the third Lord Hokage. After becoming friends with Naruto, however, his thoughts about being a Ninja change dramatically and he begins to try and improve himself. At least as far as Konohamaru goes, Naruto seems to be a better teacher than Ebisu. Ebisu may well have had some moderate successes in his time, but he is not half as much of a great teacher as he likes to make out.

See Glossary
Ebisu
Konohamaru
Hokage

The Secret Behind Rock Lee's and Might Guy's Names

The pupil Rock Lee and his master Might Guy derive their names from a couple of actors.

It is almost certain Rock Lee is named after Hong Kong action star Bruce Lee. This name was likely chosen because he specializes in Taijutsu such, as Kenpo (Kung Fu). Besides the name, you can see references to Bruce Lee in his character design too.

The name of Lee's master, Might Guy, was probably derived from Mighty Guy, the nickname of Akira Kobayashi, Japan's top action star during the 60s. Kobayashi appeared in numerous films, but in particular his early films "Guitar o Motta Wataridori" (English title: The Rambling Guitarist) and "Dynamite ni Hi o Tsukero" (lit. Light the Dynamite!) were hits, earning him the nicknames Wataridori and Mighty Guy. While his second nickname is conventionally spelled Mighty Guy in English, the "might" actually derives from the last four letters of "dynomite." It is true that Naruto creator Masashi Kishimoto had not yet been born when Kobayashi was at the apex of his popularity, but it is possible that he saw some of the charismatic actor's films. Although Kobayashi is still acting, very few people remember that he was called Mighty Guy, and even among Naruto fans many probably don't realize there is a connection.

Are Yamanaka Ino, Nara Shikamaru and Akimichi Choji really a "Dream-team"?

In their youth, the parents of Ino, Shikamaru and Choji, were known as the "Inoshikacho Trio", based on their names Yamanaka Inoichi, Nara Shikaku and Akimichi Choza. Each member of the trio had their own individual strong points, which in turn supplemented the other team members' weak points, creating a perfect balance.

For both the parents and then their children to form these perfect three-man combinations seems like too much of a coincidence to be accidental... But there is actually a reason behind it.

The word "Inoshikacho" which appears in group's name is taken from a Japanese card game called Hanafuda. The cards all have pictures of plants and animals on them and the idea is to collect matching sets or special combinations. Three of the cards have a picture of a boar, deer and butterfly drawn on them. In Japanese the characters which represent these animals (猪、鹿、蝶) are read "Ino", "Shika" and "Cho". During the game, if you collect these three cards you shout out "Yaku" and your score goes up five points.

The set up with the Inoshikacho Trio really is a bit far-fetched – each parent has a child at the age of 25, and each child is born with exactly the same skills as their parents. Masashi Kishimoto obviously came up with this as a little joke for his Japanese readers.

See Glossary
Yamanaka Ino
Nara Shikamaru
Akimichi Choji
Yamanaka Inoichi
Nara Shikaku
Akimichi Choza

Rock Lee's Urarenge (lit. Reverse Lotus) is a highly dangerous, forbidden technique. In order to perform it, it is necessary to open the Hachimontonko no Tainaimon (Eight Celestial Gates). In some cases this can lead to the death of the person performing the technique.

If you follow the system in the body through which Chakra flows, from the head down in order you have eight gates: Kaimon (Open Gate), Kyumon (Rest Gate), Seimon (Life Gate), Shomon (Wound Gate), Tomon (Shrine Gate), Keimon (View Gate), Gyomon (Surprise Gate) and Shimon (Death Gate). They act like pockets where Chakra gathers. Collectively they are known as the Hachimontonko no Tainaimon. These eight gates control the amount of Chakra flowing in the body. When Lee performs the Renge (Lotus) techniques it forcibly detaches the Chakra from this system and allows the user to summon more than ten times the amount of power than usual. The Omoterenge (Front Lotus) technique only opens up the Kaimon, but the Urarenge suppresses the brain's natural restraint, and forces the Kyumon and Seimon open. When all eight of the gates are open, for a short period it is possible to summon a power even greater than that of Lord Hokage. However, when you open all the gates you are removing a necessary natural restraint and thereby releasing a power your body is not equipped to deal with. This can easily result in death, and for this reason is designated as a forbidden art.

See Glossary

Rock Lee
Urarenge
Hachimontonko
Chakra
Omoterenge

See questions
34

The NARUTO SAGA part03

Legendary Three Ninja's Secrets

The names of the Legendary Three Ninja, Orochimaru, Jiraiya and Tsunade, originally appeared in a story called Jiraiya Goketsutan (Legend of the Gallant Jiraiya) which was written almost 200 years ago during the Edo Period.

In the story, the child of powerful clan in Kyushu becomes the pupil of an immortal from whom he is initiated into the art of frog magic. He takes the name of Jiraiya. Jiraiya then falls in love with and marries a beautiful woman named Tsunade who is skilled in snail magic. One of Jiraiya's followers is infected by a snake's venom and turns on his old master, taking the name Orochimaru. Together, Jiraiya and Tsunade try to fight against Orochimaru, but fall prey to his venom…

You can see that author Kishimoto has not just used the names from this original story, but also the animal identities of each character (frog, snake and slug). It is said in Japanese lore that when a frog, snake and slug are together in the same place a kind of deadlock is created in which none are able to move (the frog is prey to the snake, the snake is prey to the slug, and the slug is prey to the frog). There is a Japanese expression "Sansukumi" (三すくみ) which describes this state of immobility between three parties of equal power, and is still in common usage even today.

In Naruto, however, when Jiraiya's Gamabunta (giant frog), Orochimaru's Manda (giant snake) and Tsunade's Katsuyu (giant slug) meet, an epic battle ensues.

See Glossary
Orocjimaru
Jiraiya
Tsunade
Gamabunta
Manda
Katsuyu

One of Konohagakure's Legendary Three Ninja, Jiraiya doesn't seem to like being tied down to routine work such as managing the village or teaching trainee Ninja. He is a man who values his freedom, wandering from place to place and living the life he loves. His passion for the ladies, and particularly young girls, provides the source material for his romantic (or are they sexy?) novels. Jiraiya is without a doubt the author of Make Out Paradise (Viz). He is also a man of some considerable means. Naruto secretly steals his bank book and is amazed to see how much money he has saved (according to the Naruto fact book published by Shueisha, Jiraiya has several million dollars in his account). As well as Make Out Paradise Jiraiya has also written some other novels (Make Out Violence and Make Out Tactics), but surely it's not possible for him to have made this kind of money from the royalties of his books alone?! (If he had that would make him a more successful than Masashi Kishimoto himself!) He must have some other business interests...

After the third Lord Hokage dies, Jiraiya is selected as a candidate for the fifth Lord Hokage, but he turns down the offer on the basis that Tsunade is a better choice, and goes to look for her. From this we can see that Jiraiya is not indifferent to the future of the village, but doesn't want to be tied down to a nine-to-five. For a man of his means who can afford a life of leisure, there is no real need to get a job.

42 Why does Jiraiya take an interest in Naruto?

In the run up to the final part of the Chunin exams, Jiraiya decides to tutor Naruto in Ninjutsu and takes over from his regular mentor Kakashi. In a short time he initiates Naruto into the art of the Kuchiyose (Summoning) technique (Jiraiya's own specialty), and the Rasengan (Spiraling Sphere) technique that the fourth Lord Hokage pioneered. It seems that Jiraiya also wants to keep an eye on Naruto and shows a particular interest in the Fox Spirit inside him. When he looks at the markings on Naruto's belly he realizes that the fourth Lord Hokage didn't just seal in the fox spirit, but left it open enough so that Naruto would be able to use that power himself later in life (a father's gift to his son..?). Jiraiya also notices that a second seal was later added to prevent Naruto from doing so. Realizing who it was who put the second seal on Naruto's stomach, Jiraiya releases it and grants Naruto access to a new world of power.

Although the fox spirit was imprisoned in Naruto, it was not actually destroyed. The fourth Lord

Hokage's hope in sealing the spirit inside Naruto seems to have been that Naruto would one day be able to mold his and the fox's soul together. If Naruto and the spirit's soul became one and the same, then there's no way it would ever be able to escape from him, as the villagers fear. However, the possibility still remains that the fox spirit will actually end up taking over Naruto's soul. When Jiraiya removes the second seal, Naruto begins to feel that there is something else living inside him. Jiraiya stays close to Naruto watching to make sure that the spirit doesn't steal his soul and go on the rampage once again.

But what about the second seal? As Jiraiya realizes, the person who added the second seal on Naruto's body is planning to use the fox spirit for himself. This seal was intended to prevent Naruto and the fox spirit's soul having any kind of cross communication which might lead to the fox spirit's suppression. Jiraiya knows that it is in fact Orochimaru who has been making this play for Naruto's body and takes it upon himself to protect him from his old teammate.

See Glossary

Jiraiya
Hatake Kakashi
Kuchiyose
Rasengan
Hokage
Nine-Tailed Fox Spirit
Orochimaru

43 Why did Jiraiya recommend Tsunade for the position of fifth Lord Hokage?

Like Jiraiya, Tsunade was a pupil of the third Lord Hokage. She was also formerly a member of his team and is the one person he can really trust. Jiraiya feels that her bright, cheerful character is just what the village needs after the dark events that brought about the death of the third Lord Hokage, and that Konohagakure would benefit from her prodigious medical skills. Tsunade is also the granddaughter of the original Lord Hokage. As explained in earlier, the rules state that to become Lord Hokage, candidates must get the recommendation of several different Jonin. While the blood link is not strictly speaking necessary, it does have a large influence on the selection process.

Like Jiraiya, Tsunade has left the village for a life of wandering, but accepts the offer of the position, because she knows Jiraiya, and she knows that he wouldn't ask her if he weren't completely serious. If the offer hadn't come from directly from him, though, she may well have turned it down.

See Glossary
Jiraiya
Tsunade
Hokage
Konohagakure

See questions
18

The Historical Ninja

Naruto's story is set in a universe inhabited by Ninja, but the picture it paints is very different from Japan's historical Ninja, and much has been dramatized.

Japan's Ninja were a military group that existed mainly between 1200 and 1600, a time during which Japan had not yet become a unified country. Each region was controlled by a Daimyo, or feudal lord, and war engulfed the land.

Although the Ninja are classified as a military group, the actual battles were fought by men with swords, the Samurai or Bushi. The work of the Ninja was almost exclusively focused on espionage. Rather than fight, their training emphasized fleeing to ensure they would avoid being killed and return to their masters with any information they gathered. Therefore, Ninja didn't wear any armor or carry heavy weapons, which might impede their agility. Shuriken, Kunai and other Ningu (Ninja tools) were carried not for combat, but to aid in escaping.

They often operated at night and wore black so they would be harder to see. The Ninja were also involved in scientific and technological research. As they often had to travel long distances on missions, they developed the Ganyaku (a small, high calorie pill) and carefully researched edible and medicinal plants.

They really did have techniques called Ninjutsu, like the Ninja in Naruto, but as the Ninja themselves were spies who stole information for a living, they were very careful not to let their secrets be discovered. Therefore, they passed on all their techniques orally. As a result, no written records of their techniques exist, so how they worked is still a mystery.

44 What is Jiraiya's Ninja ranking? Chunin? Jonin?

Not much is known about Jiraiya's past. We know that he was in the same year as Orochimaru and Tsunade (now aged 50), that he was the pupil of the third Lord Hokage and that he graduated from the Ninja Academy and became a Genin at the age of six. With this kind of resume it seems more than likely he was selected to become a Jonin, but in the Naruto fact books published by Shueisha there is nothing explicitly stated about his rank.

When the fourth Lord Hokage was being selected, Orochimaru put himself up for the position, so we know that he was a Jonin, but the same kind of background information is not provided in the case of Jiraiya. We are also never told exactly when he started his travels as a wandering hermit.

When the position for fifth Lord Hokage becomes vacant Jiraiya is singled out not just by the Konohagakure Jonin, but also by the feudal lord of the Land of Fire. From this we can assume that he is a Jonin, but since he has been traveling and writing racy novels for such a long time, he might have lost some of his edge as a Ninja.

See Glossary

Jiraiya
Genin
Chunin
Jonin
Orochimaru
Tsunade
Hokage
Ninja Academy

45 When did Jiraiya start his travels?

Given the fact that young Ninja like Naruto have never met Jiraiya we can assume that he left the village of Konohagakure at least ten years before the beginning of the story. The fourth Lord Hogake died just after Naruto was born, and Naruto is now 13, which means that the fourth Lord Hokage took up the post more than 13 years previously.

Around the time Kakashi gets the Sharingan (during the Battle of the Kannabi Bridge), the young fourth Lord Hokage makes an appearance. At this stage he is the Jonin instructor for Kakashi's team, which means this happens before he becomes the fourth Lord Hokage. Kakashi is not portrayed as being especially young, so this episode can't be very far in the past. Kakashi is now 26 years old. Since, by this point, Kakashi's teacher had not yet become the fourth Lord Hokage and Kakashi can't have been any younger than ten, the Battle of the Kannabi Bridge must have taken place no more than 16 years previously.

Straight after this battle Kakashi's teacher

becomes the fourth Lord Hokage. When the Ninja of Konohagakure are choosing the new head of the village there is no talk of Jiraiya or Tsunade, even though they are both outstanding Ninja and suitable candidates for the job. This suggests that they had already left the village by this point(ie.16 or more years before).

Jiraiya was the fourth Lord Hokage's teacher, which means he can't have left the village a very long time before then (for example 30 years ago, when he was aged 20). What is certain, though, is that if he had been around, Jiraiya would not have let the fourth Lord Hokage take on the Fox Spirit on his own.

S ee Glossary
Jiraiya
Konohagakure
Hatake Kakashi
Sharingan
Kannabi Bridge

See questions
25

46 Jiraiya seems to be a big fan of the ladies. Doesn't he have a wife?

Jiraiya is portrayed as a lovable pervert, who has a soft spot for young ladies. He even steals money from Naruto's wallet (despite his enormous personal wealth) so that he can entertain a woman at a bar! Jiraiya's love of women started at an early age when he developed the Toshijutsu (X-Ray vision) in order to spy on the women bathing at the public baths…

When Jiraiya re-meets Tsunade and asks her to be the fifth Lord Hokage, at first she turns his offer down. He asks her to remember their past together, which leads to a discussion about the time she refused his proposal of marriage. Jiraiya appears to still be in love Tsunade and has carried the pain of rejection around with him ever since that time. For Jiraiya, Tsunade is the only woman he'll ever love and this is the root cause of his bachelor life-style. His casual philandering is just a way of distracting himself from his feelings towards her.

See Glossary
Jiraiya
Tsunade

47 Why is Tsunade called the Densetsu no Kamo?

Tsunade is crazy about gambling and even wears a Kimono with the Chinese character for "Bet" (賭) printed on the back. While being the most dedicated, she is also one of the most unlucky gamblers in town and among her gambling associates she is known as the Densetsu no Kamo (Sitting Duck).

Even though she constantly loses, she never gives up and borrows money to fuel her habit. Her debts run into several millions of dollars! She also has a tendency to run out on her debtors without paying up. By using transformation techniques Tsunade changes her appearance from a woman in her fifties to a woman in her twenties or thirties to keep one step ahead of the various money-lenders (both legal and illegal) that she owes money to.

So just what happened to those millions of dollar's worth of debt when Tsunade became Lord Hokage? The position of Lord Hokage is an important public office and a scandal involving money would draw criticism from other countries and hurt the village's image just like in real-life politics.

We can only assume that these debts were settled up in some way. Either that or the money lenders didn't realize it was Tsunade they were looking for and are even now searching for the whereabouts of the Sitting Duck. It doesn't seem in Tsunade's nature to abuse her position of power to write off her debts, but you never know…

See Glossary
Tsunade
Densetsu no Kamo
Hokage

48 Tsunade gets the shakes whenever she sees blood. Is she really fit to be a Ninja?

Tsunade is a Ninja skilled in the arts of healing. She has had plenty of experience dealing with blood both on the battlefield and in the hospital where she performs surgical operations. You'd think a doctor who shakes at the sight of blood can't be much good at their job.

When she loses her younger brother Nawaki and the man she loves, Dan, on the battlefield it has a deeply traumatic effect on her. In the case of Dan, Tsunade was actually part of the medical team trying to save his life. Dan's internal organs had ruptured and Tsunade had to put her finger inside his body in order to try and heal him. In the end, it was too late and Dan died. Ever since then, whenever she sees blood it reminds her of the feeling of Dan's blood on her finger. Tsunade is only too aware that going into a panic at the sight of blood is a major failing in a Ninja. It was perhaps around this time that she decided to quit the village and immerse herself in gambling.

Tsunade's lover Dan seems to have died not long after her younger brother Nawaki. Nawaki died when he was 12 years old, so how old was she at the time?

Tsunade and her brother are fairly far apart in age. If we assume that there is a gap of ten years between them, then Tsunade was 22 when Nawaki died and 23 when Dan died. She is now 50, which means this all happened at least 27 years before. In fact it is quite likely this took place even longer ago than that. If this is the case, then Tsunade would have left the village and gone wandering about 30 years ago.

When Tsunade meets Naruto, he helps her to overcome her phobia of blood. Only then is she able to be a Ninja once more and take up the position of fifth Lord Hokage.

See Glossary
Tsunade
Nawaki
Dan
Hokage

The Ninpo Sozosaisei (lit. Creation Rebirth Technique) that Tsunade performs is a kind of healing technique. It is highly advanced and can be used to heal even the deepest of wounds. At first glance it doesn't seem particularly dangerous. The technique involves rapidly speeding up the body's rate of cell division in order to rejuvenate the wounded body tissue. When this technique is performed, a wound that would normally take a month to heal, can heal in just a few minutes. There is a limit, however, to the number of times a human's cells can divide in their lifetime. By speeding up the process unnaturally, it can bring on aging and results in a shortening of life span. In cases when the injury is serious enough to be fatal this technique can be used on the area around the wound to actually remake body tissue. To do this, the user must speed up the body's cell division to extreme levels. This leads to an even greater shortening of life span. For Tsunade, who is already 50 years old, it is especially dangerous to use this technique on her own body. Even if she is able to heal her wound, there is a very real possibility she could bring on her own death. For this reason the Ninpo Sozosaisei is categorized as a forbidden technique.

See Glossary
Tsunade
Sozosaisei

50 Why did Orochimaru leave the village of Konohagakure?

Before the beginning of the story, Orochimaru leaves the village of Konohagakure and establishes the village of Otogakure in a nearby country. During the Chunin exams, he tries to destroy the village of Konohagakure by staging a coup d'etat. The reason why Orochimaru leaves the village of Konohagakure in the first place is because he believed he should have been chosen for the position of fourth Lord Hokage. Bitter at being passed over he builds his own village so that he can be the boss. This does not seem to quench his thirst for power, however, and he continues to hanker after the fame that comes with the rank of Lord Hokage. In a sense he has still not completely abandoned Konohagakure.

For a long time Orochimaru has been researching the secrets of immortality, a field which is strictly forbidden in the world of Ninja (the discovery that he was doing this research was the original reason he couldn't become Lord Hokage). His ambition is to learn the secret of immortality and use it to help him take over the world. Orochimaru's desire to destroy Konohagakure is similar to the feeling of Sasuke's older brother, Itachi, who tries to kill his whole family because they are holding him back from realizing his true power. But more than that, Orochimaru feels slighted by the Ninja of Konohagakure who would not accept him as their leader. By terrorizing the village, he wants to prove that he is the strongest of all.

See Glossary

Orochimaru
Konohagakure
Chunin exams
Hokage
Uchiha Sasuke
Uchiha Itachi

See questions
23

51 Why does an evil character like Orochimaru have so many followers?

Orochimaru has managed to amass quite a number of followers in the Otogakure village, and even has Kabuto from Konohagakure working undercover for him. These young, impressionable Ninja are dazzled by his skills and aspire to his awesome power. There are some, like Sasuke and the Oto no Yoninshu (Sound 4) – Kidomaru, Shirobo, Sakon and Tayuya – who have been infected by Orochimaru's Juin (Cursed Seal), but most willingly chose to follow him, enchanted by the prospect of the great power they can gain.

Kabuto has entered and failed the Chunin selection exams six times posing as a candidate from village of Konohagakure and has been using the exams as a means of spying for Orochimaru. While he maintains an image as a loser, Kabuto is in fact a very powerful Ninja. There is no detailed explanation as to why Kabuto is drawn to Orochimaru, but it seems that he admires his audacity and strength of will.

See Glossary
Orochimaru
Otogakure
Yakushi Kabuto

See questions
55

52 Why doesn't Orochimaru hide the body of Lord Kazekage after he kills him?

Orochimaru planned to use the Chunin exams as an opportunity to overthrow the village of Konohagakure. As part of this plan, Orochimaru assassinates the leader of the village of Sunagakure, Lord Kazekage, transforms into him and then appears at the tournament site in his place. After assassinating Lord Kazekage, instead of trying to hide the body, Orochimaru leaves it where it is. If someone had discovered the body, Orchimaru's cover would have been blown and the whole plan would have failed. So why does he do this?

Orochimaru is a crazed egocentric, with a chip on his shoulder about not being accepted as Lord Hokage. Showing the world that he had triumphed over the mighty Lord Kazekage is more important to him than the success of his plan. If he had hidden the body no one would have ever known how or why Lord Kazekage had disappeared.

Although Orochimaru then attempts to overthrow Konohagakure, the overall damage is far from devastating. Maybe his real purpose was just to take out the third Lord Hokage (bringing his tally of defeated Kage up to two). By doing this he could show the world his awesome power.

See Glossary

Orochimaru
Kazekage
Hokage

53 What kind of technique is Orochimaru's Edotensei ?

The Edotensei (lit. Impure World Resurrection) is a forbidden form of Kuchiyose technique in which dead souls are brought back to life. To perform this technique it is necessary to sacrifice living people in order to house the dead souls. Orochimaru uses the Edotesei technique to summon the souls of the first and second Lord Hokage and makes them fight against the third Lord Hokage. When the souls are called back from the dead they still have all their memories from their previous lives, but, because of the incredible power of the Jutsu, have no choice but to obey. This is true even in the case of Ninja like the first Lord Hokage. He may be able to remember all of his techniques, but he is powerless to resist.

There is another technique similar to this called the Fushitensei (lit. Living Corpse Resurrection) technique. Orochimaru uses the Fushitensei to move his soul from one person's body to another. By repeating this technique he is able to avoid aging and live indefinitely. Once a person's body is taken over in this way, their soul is destroyed. Orochimaru has sacrificed many lives perfecting this technique in pursuit of his goal of immortality. The only limitation on the Fushitensei is that once a new host body has been occupied, it is not possible to transmigrate to another body for a few years.

S ee Glossary

Orochimaru
Kuchiyose Edotensei
Hokage

54 | Why does Orochimaru have his eye on Sasuke's body?

Having perfected the Fushitensei, all Orochimaru has to do in order to achieve immortality is to keep moving bodies. The next body that he has in his sights is Sasuke's. What attracts Orochimaru most to Sasuke's body is the Sharingan. This is a special hereditary ability unique to the Uchiha Clan, so the only way Orochimaru can get it is by physically implanting an eye from an Uchiha Clan member (as Kakashi does), or by using the transmigration technique to move into Sasuke's body. Since Orochimaru has already perfected the Fushitensei, there is no need to go to the bother of pulling out Sasuke's eye.

See Glossary
Orochimaru
Uchiha Sasuke
Uchiha Clan
Sharingan

See questions
11

55 Are the members of the Oto no Yoninshu human?

Orochimaru's elite team of bodygaurds is known as the Oto no Yoninshu (Sound 4), and each member has their own strange features or special tricks: Kidomaru has six arms; Jirobo can suck up his opponent's Chakra; Tayuya has antlers growing from her head; and Sakon and Ukon are two people who can unite in one body. The Sound 4, however, were not born with these unusual abilities, but acquired them as a result of the Juin (Cursed Seal) that Orochimaru has placed on them. This Seal is so powerful that it can even transform flesh. The Sound 4 are controlled by this Juin and must do everything that Oroshimaru asks them to, but as a reward they gain a power which is beyond any human's.

See Glossary

Orochimaru
Kidomaru
Jirobo
Sakon
Tayuya
Juinjutsu

56 Is Kimimaro different to the other Oto Ninja?

Orochimaru's full team of bodyguards consists of five members: the Oto no Yoninshu (Sound 4) and Kimimaro. Together they make up the Oto no Goninshu (Sound 5). The single remaining member of the Kaguya Clan, Kimimaro keeps slightly apart from Sound 4 on account of a terminal illness he has contracted. Orochimaru seems to have a special place in his heart for both Kimimaro and Sasuke, which is reflected in the Juin he uses on them; Kimimaro is given a Chi no Juin (lit. Earth Cursed Seal), while Sasuke is given a Ten no Juin (lit. Heaven Cursed Seal). Kimimaro possesses the special Kekkeigenkai of the Kaguya Clan called Shikotsumyaku (lit. Corpse Bone Pulse), which gives him the abnormal ability to grow antler-like bones from any part of his body, which can be used to stab an opponent during battle (he can even take the bones out of his body). Orochimaru is keen to use this technique for himself and would have almost certainly moved into Kimimaro's body if it hadn't been for his illness.

Until he becomes sick, Kimimaro's reason for living has been to offer Orochimaru his body. When he realizes this dream will not come true, he decides that, at the very least, he will deliver Sasuke's body to Orochimaru with his own hands. When Shikamaru and his rescue team come to get Sasuke back, Kimimaro makes a last spirited stand against them.

See Glossary

Kimimaro
Orochimaru
Kekkeigenkai
Uchiha Sasuke
Nara Shikamaru

57 What is the shadowy organization Akatsuki that Orochimaru belonged to?

A Akatsuki is an organization made up of nine Ninja, including Uchiha Itachi and Hoshigaki Kisame. All of the members of Akatsuki are ranked as S level criminals. The status of the organization and its purpose are for now unknown, but the fact that are trying to get hold of the immense power of the Fox and Shukaku spirit suggests that they are planning something big. At one time Orochimaru was also a member of Akatsuki. Given that it is a secret organization it is a little strange that they let Orochimaru leave so easily. By his own admission Orochimaru is no match for Itachi, so if they wanted to they would have no problem taking him out.

In all probability Orochimaru and Akatsuki have some kind of secret pact... Perhaps Orochimaru's assassination of Kazekage and Hokage fitted in with Akatsuki's plans. If so, then it seems likely that they are planning to stage some kind of coup d'etat.

See Glossary

Akatsuki
Orochimaru
Uchiha Itachi
Hoshigaki Kisame
Nine-Tailed Fox Spirit
Kazekage
Hokage

During one dramatic episode Orochimaru, Jiraiya and Tsunade each summon their respective animals (Manda, Gamabunta and Katsuyu) by Kuchiyose, and an enormous battle ensues. The battle, however, finishes with no clear winner. If the Legendary Three Ninja were all to fight each other one-on-one, who would come out the strongest?

Although Jiraiya is recommended for the position of Lord Hokage, he turns it down in the interests of the village and offers the job to Tsunade. We know that he cares deeply for the future of Konohagakure, so by entrusting the position of Lord Hokage to Tsunade, he is basically conceding that she is equal to, if not more skilled than him.

Orochimaru rates Itachi's skills higher than his own, while Itachi is so in awe of Jiraiya that he wouldn't take him on even if he had Hoshigaki Kisame to back him up.

Taking Itachi as a gauge, we can calculate that Jiraiya is a few levels above Orochimaru. If we then consider how highly Jiraiya rates Tsunade there is only one conclusion: Tsunade is the strongest.

Unless you actually put them all in a ring together it would be hard to say who would really win, but by this reckoning it certainly seems that Tsunade was the right choice to be the fifth Lord Hokage.

59 Who is the strongest character in Naruto?

Going purely on what the different characters say and think and the results of the various fights, we can draw the following conclusion: The third Lord Hokage is rated as the strongest Lord Hokage in history, as well as the strongest Ninja in all of the Five Great Countries.

Even though he is old at the time, the third Lord Hokage is defeated by Orochimaru, which means that Orochimaru is stronger still. Orochimaru rates Sasuke's brother Itachi above himself, while Itachi feels he is no match for Jiraiya. Jiraiya in turn considers Tsunade his equal if not superior.

This all suggests that Tsunade is the strongest, but there is one Ninja who is said to be the greatest of all: Hatake Sakumo. Otherwise known as White Fang, Kakashi's father Sakumo was a Ninja of extraordinary skill. According to Uchiha Obito, even the Legendary Three Ninja pale in comparison to him. Undefeated in battle, the only person who could kill White Fang was himself.

⑤ee Glossary

Hokage
Five Great Countries
Orochimaru
Jiraiya
Tsunade
Uchiha Itachi
Hatake Sakumo
Uchiha Obito

See questions
58

The NARUTO SAGA

part04

Rivals' Secrets

60 What kind of a person is Gato?

Naruto's first assignment after being promoted to a C rank Ninja is to look after Tazuna, the bridge builder. The team must escort him back to his country (the Land of Waves) and protect him until the bridge is completed. In this episode Naruto gets his first taste of the big wide world outside the village. From the start Tazuna knows that there are Ninja trying to assassinate him, but he hides this information when he asks the village of Konohagakure for protection (regular protection by C rank Ninja does not cost much money, but protection from Ninja assassins is the work of B rank Ninja and the rate is much higher). The Ninja hired to kill Tazuna have been paid for by the enormously wealthy shipping company owner Gato. The shipping company is actually a legitimate front for his illegal activities. Using gangs of thugs and Ninja to provide the muscle, he runs drug smuggling operations and extortion rackets, taking over other companies by force. He has for some time been tightly controlling the transport routes to the weak and virtually defenseless Land of Waves (which has no Ninja) with a view to taking over the country himself. For Gato, the bridge to the mainland which is under construction represents a threat to his control over the island. Once there is a land route to the Land of Waves, Gato will no longer be able to control the flow of traffic to and from other countries, so he decides to have Tazuna assassinated.

Ninja existed in Japan around more than four hundred years ago, but in the fictional world of Naruto, the cultural setting in some ways more closely resembles the present day. In addition to the TVs and mobile phones that occasionally crop up, Gato's business practices (acquisitions and mergers) have a distinctly modern feel to them. The Ninja that go AWOL from their villages seem to gravitate towards these powerful men and often end up becoming their private bodyguards.

See Glossary
Gato
Tazuna
Konohagakure

61 Why is Zabuza involved with Gato's operations?

Z abuza is a ruthless Ninja known as the Kirigakure no Kijin (lit. Demon Man), whose notoriety has spread far and wide. While he was still living in Kirigakure, he was a member of the Anbu unit and took part in many assassinations. Each operation was a success on account of his deadly Silent Killing technique. A few years before the beginning of the story he attempts to overthrow Kirigakure with some other Ninja from the village, but fails. He then leaves Kirigakure and goes into hiding. Some time soon after that he hooks up with Gato and his gang.

A very proud Ninja who looks down on everyone else, Zabuza surely doesn't consider Gato anything more than a client and it can only really have been his wealth that attracted him to Gato in the first place. Perhaps Zabuza has not completely given up on the idea of taking the village of Kirigakure for himself and is using Gato as a convenient way to raise money.

It seems that he has also been using Haku purely for his own ends, but when they are lying side by side on the point of death we see another side to his character and he even sheds a tear or two for his devoted companion.

While he may have failed in his attempt to take Kirigakure by force and been seduced by the power of Gato's money, Zabuza maintains his integrity as a Ninja until the very end. He needs money to further ambitions, but he never "sells-out" to Gato.

See Glossary
Momochi Zabuza
Kirigakure no Kijin
Silent Killing
Gato
Haku

62 What is the Shukaku spirit that is living inside Gaara?

Gaara is created by Lord Kazekage as a kind of secret weapon to strengthen the village of Sunagakure. While he is still inside his mother Lord Kazekage implants a spirit known as Shukaku in Gaara's body (Shukaku was the spirit of an old monk which had been sealed in a teakettle for many years). Gaara's mother dies after giving birth as a result of this process.

Initially the Shukaku spirit is referred to in the story as Suna no Keshin (lit. Incarnation of Sand). Gaara always carries a gourd filled with sand on his back and it is this sand which protects him during battle. Because the Incarnation of Sand is living inside Gaara's body, whenever he comes under attack, the sand protects him of its own accord, sometimes without him even realizing it (this makes surprise attacks on Gaara meaningless). The first kanji in the name Shukaku (守鶴) also appears in the verb "to protect" (Mamoru: 守る).

In addition to being the Incarnation of Sand, the Shukaku spirit is also presented in the series as being the spirit of an old monk from Sunagakure.

In translation it's not so clear, but the Japanese word used to mean "spirit" in this case (生き霊) refers specifically to a soul which has temporarily left the body of a living person (生 means "alive" or "living"). If you go by the literal meaning of the word then that means the old monk of Sunagakure is still living somewhere, but he doesn't make an appearance at any point in the story. In this case, it seems that Masashi Kishimoto is using the word "spirit" to refer to the "living" soul of a dead monk.

But isn't Shukaku some kind of animal..? As the story progresses, it turns out that Shukaku is actually a Tanuki ("Raccoon Dog" in English) which has been implanted in Gaara in a similar way to the fox spirit which is sealed in Naruto's belly. That makes Shukaku an incarnation of sand, an old monk and a raccoon dog all at the same time… The name Shukaku also contains the character for a type of bird called Tsuru (鶴) in Japanese ("Crane" in English). How does this all link up?

In Japanese folklore, the raccoon dog, like the fox, is said to be skilled at transforming its appearance. While foxes are traditionally associated with the female form, raccoon dogs are said to be able to transform themselves into men. Perhaps this raccoon dog spirit had been posing as an old monk before somebody from the village of Sunagakure (Lord Kazekage?) sealed him inside a teakettle. If we go with this interpretation then the true identity of Shukaku is the raccoon dog. You could then say that the reason why the alternative name "Incarnation of Sand" exists is because this raccoon dog spirit is skilled at Yojutsu (Spirit Techniques) which involve sand.

In long serializations like Naruto it is not uncommon for little inconsistencies in the details of the setting to arise. It is possible that Shukaku started off as an old monk and then changed to the raccoon dog along the way. The main point here, though, is the fact that Shukaku was sealed in a teakettle. In Japan there is a famous story called "Bunbuku Chakama" about a raccoon dog inside a teakettle. Masashi Kishimoto is almost certainly referencing that story in this part of the Naruto series. Therefore, from the start, he intended Shukaku to be a raccoon dog spirit. The old monk must have been a disguise that the raccoon dog spirit was using.

See Glossary
Gaara
Shukaku
Kazekage
Sunagakure
Suna no Keshin

See questions
63 65

63 Why does Gaara kill people for no reason?

Deliberately created as weapon for the Sunagakure village, Gaara grows up without the support of a normal, loving family, and lives life not knowing what his purpose in the world is. Even though Lord Kazekage is his father, he begins to fear Gaara's destructive potential, and at the tender age of six tries to have him assassinated (all those who try perish Gaara's hand). Around this time Gaara's outlook on life takes a turn for the worse and he decides that his one purpose for living is to kill other people.

There are times, however, when Gaara tries to kill people without even meaning to. After the second part of the Chunin exams he steals into Rock Lee's hospital room and tries to kill him while he is sleeping. There is no good reason to kill Lee and Gaara himself doesn't even know why he is doing it. It would seem that the Shukaku spirit inside his body has taken control of him, and is using him as an instrument of death against his own will.

See Glossary

Gaara
Sunagakure
Kazekage
Shukaku
Chunin exams
Rock Lee

See questions
62 65

64 Did Gaara really never love anyone?

In his infancy Gaara adored Yashamaru who looked after him like a surrogate mother. Despite having raised him, Yashamaru was the first person Lord Kazekage had try and assassinate Gaara. As a result of this incident Gaara decided never to trust or love anyone again and he hardened his heart to world around him. This didn't mean, however, that he never loved anyone at all after that. In spite of the fact that Lord Kazekage was trying to kill him and even sending assassins to do the job, it seems that Gaara still loved him. Well, maybe "love" is putting it a bit strongly, but he certainly didn't hate him. Even though Gaara thinks nothing of killing, and probably has many chances, never tries to kill Lord Kazekage. When Lord Kazekage and Orochimaru join forces to topple the village of Konohagakure, he willingly obeys the order from his father to attend the Chunin exams. Perhaps simply because of the bond of blood between them, Gaara has a feeling of filial loyalty and thanks to the father who brought him into the world.

See Glossary
Gaara
Yashamaru
Kazekage
Orochimaru
Konohagakure

See questions
66

65 Why is it that Gaara's body sometimes changes?

Gaara has had the Shukaku spirit sealed inside him since before he was born. While Naruto has some whisker-like markings on his face and slightly pronounced canines, the Fox Spirit imprisoned inside him never fully takes possession of his soul, so never goes as far as transforming his body in any radical way. In Gaara's case, however, he is sometimes unable to control the Shukaku spirit and it occasionally takes possession of his body. At these times physical transformations occur. Given that Lord Kazekage, who brought Gaara into the world, considers him dangerous enough to try and have him assassinated, it is clear that the people around him also realize that he is not always able to control the Shukaku spirit.

Gaara is a member of a team of three Ninja along with Temari and Kankuro. Unlike Naruto, Sasuke and Sakura, they do not carry out duties under the supervision of an instructor. Temari is Gaara's older sister and Kankuro is Gaara's older brother. Putting these siblings together in a team is Lord

See Glossary

Gaara
Shukaku
Kazekage
Temari
Kankuro
Uchiha Sasuke
Haruno Sakura

See questions
62 65

125

Kazekage's way of keeping an eye on Gaara to make sure he doesn't go completely out of control.

Yashamaru was the one person who showed Gaara any affection when he was a young child and looked after him like a mother. How could she have brought herself to try and assassinate him? Admittedly the order came from the head of the village, who also happened to be Gaara's father, but it still seems strange that she actually went through with it...

Yashamaru is in fact Gaara's aunt on his mother's side. When Gaara was still inside his mother she had the Shukaku spirit implanted in her and her life was sacrificed in order to bring Gaara into the world. Does Gaara's aunt still hold a grudge against him for causing the death of her sister?

This seems a bit unfair; Gaara didn't personally choose to have the Shukaku spirit implanted in him, and he certainly wouldn't have wanted to take his own mother's life. If anything Gaara is also a victim in this scenario. The person who planned the whole thing was his father Lord Kazekage, so really Yashamaru's anger should be directed at him. Nevertheless, when Lord

Kazekage gives her the order to assassinate Gaara, she attempts to carry it out.

It seems that Yashamaru is motivated not out of bitterness towards Gaara, but out of a combination of love and fear. As the person closest to him, she has had more chance than anyone to observe the evil that lurks within Gaara's soul and she fears that if he is let out into the world he will become a very dangerous person. If Gaara must be assassinated, as Yashamaru has come to believe, then she, who has loved him and raised him as her son, should be the one to take his life.

S ee Glossary
Gaara
Yashamaru
Shukaku
Kazekage

See questions
64

Accrding to the Naruto official data pack, Temari is ranked as a Genin. She goes round in a group of three along with her two brothers Kankuro and Gaara, always keeping an eye on Gaara to make sure he doesn't do anything too crazy. Lord Kazekage orders the three of them to take part in the Chunin exams as part of a larger scheme to overthrow the village of Konohagakure, which he has been cooking up with Orochimaru. As such, her main reason for entering is not really to become a Chunin.

The exams are also judged in such a way that winning the final tournament is no guarantee of selection. What the judges are looking at is the kind of attitude each Genin displays, their approach to the tasks they are given and their strategies for dealing with whatever situation they find themselves in. So even though Temari wins in a one-on-one fight during the tournament, the judges are impressed with Shikamaru's tactical thinking and select him as a Chunin.

That said, it still seems a little unfair on Temari. During her fight with Shikamaru she makes good use of her special techniques, in particular the Kamaitachi no Jutsu (lit. Cutting Whirlwind Technique) which is both a defensive and offensive move, and her Kirikirimai (lit. Cutting Dance) Kuchiyose technique, which is powerful enough to destroy a whole forest. Shikamaru never gives the impression of having the tactical upper hand, and Temari's powers of analysis seem to be just as strong as his.

The fact that Temari remains a Genin suggests that the criteria for being selected as a Chunin differ between the villages of Konohagakure and Sunagakure, or that Sunagakure Ninja are expected to reach a higher standard. Whatever the reason, there is a good case to be made for saying that Temari was unfairly robbed of the title.

🄢ee Glossary

Temari
Nara Shikamaru
Chunin
Kankuro
Gaara
Kazekage
Chunin exams
Orochimaru
Genin
Kamaitachi no Jutsu
Kirikirimai
Kuchiyose
Sungakure

Kankuro specializes in techniques which involve puppets and he is always carrying at least one around on his back with him. Sometimes, however, it is not the puppet that is riding on his back, but the other way round – what seems at first to be the puppet is actually Kankuro himself. By hitching a ride on its back, Kankuro can travel in comfort while the puppet does all the work.

At other times, he seals his puppets in a scroll using a Fuin (Sealing) technique. Whenever he needs to use them, he can summon them from the scroll using a Kuchiyose-style technique. This makes the puppets light and easy to carry around.

But why does Kankuro use puppets in the first place? Gaara and Temari's special skills both relate closely to the natural environment of the country they grew up in (Gaara with his sand techniques and Temari with her wind techniques). At first glance Kankuro's puppets seem to have no relation to his place of origin, but this is not the case. In former times a puppet maker called

Akasuna no Sasori lived in the village of Sunagakure. He was a master craftsman and through his influence puppet-Ninjutsu grew in popularity and became a unique specialty of the village. Sunagakure even has a unit known as the Kugutsu Butai (lit. Puppet Unit).

See Glossary
Kankuro
Gaara
Kuchiyose

69 How does Jirobo suck out his opponent's Chakra?

Jirobo has a special technique called Dotonkekkai Dorodomu (lit. Earth Release Barrier: Dungeon Chamber of Nothingness) which he uses to suck out his opponent's Chakra. Various different techniques for draining Chakra appear throughout Naruto, but these usually involve direct, physical contact. By using the Dotonkekkai Dorodomu technique Jirobo traps his opponent in a dome of earth and then sucks out all their Chakra without ever getting close enough to put himself in danger.

Once inside the dome of earth, Chakara flows out of the opponent's body like sweat and is transmitted by some unknown medium into Jirobo's body (perhaps there is some kind of Chakra-sucking element in the air inside the dome?).

Jirobo is quite a big guy, so generally consumes a lot of stamina. Chakra comes from stamina, so someone with a big body like Jirobo needs to find ways to keep up their levels if they are going to perform Ninjutsu techniques (Akimchi Choji does this by eating and taking special power-up pills).

The Dotonkekkai Dorodomu is ideal for Jirobo in this respect, because it allows him maximum Chakra at minimum effort.

See Glossary
Jirobo
Dotonkekkai Dorodomu
Chakra

70 Does Kidomaru's Kumosenkyu Suzaku really have an accuracy of 120% as he claims?

Kidomaru's secret weapon is the Kumosenkyu Suzaku (lit. Spider War Bow Tremendous Fissure), which is an archery-style technique, but with a slight twist. Kidomaru has the special ability to produce thread and Kumonenkin (lit. Spider Sticky Gold) from his mouth like a spider. This Kumonenkin is a viscous fluid which hardens like metal and which he uses to make his arrows (and possibly bow?). After he has made an arrow, he then produces a thread from his mouth which he attaches to the arrow and fires at the enemy. The thread is connected to his mouth so he is able to transmit Chakra along it and change the course of the arrow in mid-flight. This means that if his opponent tries to dodge, the arrow will still find its mark every time. During the Chunin exams even quick-footed Hyuga Neji is unable to avoid getting hit. Kidomaru's accuracy rate of 120% is no exaggeration.

See Glossary

Kidomaru
Kumosenkyu Suzaku
Kumonenkin
Chunin exams
Hyuga Neji

Known for being a great flute player, Tayuya combines her hobby with a unique form of Genjutsu in which she attacks her opponent's sense of hearing. Most Genjutsu are used to distort the opponent's visual senses (often in the form of hallucinations) and require some kind of face to face contact. The Sharingan Saiminjutsu (Hypnosis Technique) is a good example of this. In order for it to work effectively, the user must have direct eye contact with their opponent. Tayuya's flute technique is a rare form of Genjutsu which works on the sense of hearing. Because of the way sound travels she is able to use it even when he is hidden from view.

When a Ninja is trying to locate a hidden enemy he or she will normally listen out for any kind of sound that might give away the enemy's location. At these times the Ninja will focus all their concentration on their sense of hearing. This, however, makes them doubly susceptible to Genjutsu which work on that sense. If the opponent stops up their ears to prevent the effect of the Jutsu, then they become unable to pinpoint their enemy's location.

Sound travels in all directions at once, which means that that this technique is effective regardless of the enemy's position. Shikamaru experiences Tayuya's flute Genjutsu first hand when he goes to rescue Sasuke and has a hard time extricating himself.

See Glossary

Tayuya
Genjutsu
Sharingan
Nara Shikamaru
Uchiha Sasuke

72 Why are Sakon and Ukon able to join and separate their bodies?

Twin brothers Ukon and Sakon normally share one body, but they can also separate into two bodies and fight independently of each other. This is because their bodies have the special ability to breakdown and rebuild cells and protein using Chakra. By remodeling their cells they are able to match each other's body tissue and separate or join together at will.

By the same token, this unusual ability also allows the brothers to remodel their cell structure and join bodies with complete strangers. The one draw back with this is that when they join un unknown person's body, they temporarily share that person's nervous system. This means that if the person they have joined bodies with were to suffer any kind of injury while they were in that state, they would also be able to feel the pain.

See Glossary
Sakon Ukon
Chakra

What kind of Ninja is Akatsuki member Hoshigaki Kisame?

Originally a Ninja from the village of Kirigakure, Hoshigaki Kisame is an unsavory character with a fierce-looking mouth, expressionless eyes and a sword longer than his own body.

Of all the Ninja wanted for crimes in each of the countries in Naruto's world, Hoshigaki Kisame is considered one of the most dangerous. Ranked an S level criminal, he is said to have been involved in many subversive acts including the assassination of a feudal lord.

Judging by how obediently he follows orders from Itachi, Hoshigaki Kisame seems to be a loyal character who, once sworn to an organization, will obey all commands from above unquestioningly. This suggest that the heinous crimes he has committed in his past were under orders from some kind of higher power (although there are no clear details about this given in the series).

Like Hoshigaki, Zabuza is another Ninja who has left the village of Kirigakure and is wanted by the law. In the past the Kirigakure Ninja Academy employed a ruthless system, whereby in order to graduate, students had to prove themselves in a fight to the death with their fellow classmates. One year Zabuza massacred more than 100 students, so the village authorities decided to reform the system. While undoubtedly producing many highly skilled Ninja, it seems that the education policy in Kirigakure has a tendency to instill a certain blood-lust and ruthless ambition in its students that contrasts sharply with the values of teamwork and friendship cherished by the Konohagakure Ninja Academy. This tendency is apparent in Hoshigaki Kisame, Zabuza and the Kiri no Shinobigatana Shichi Ninshu (lit. Seven Ninja Blades of Kirigakure), all of whom have left the village in pursuit of their own ambitions.

S ee Glossary

Akatsuki
Hoshigaki Kisame
Uchiha Itachi
Momochi Zabuza
Kirigakure
Konohagakure

The Secret Life of Masashi Kishimoto

Masashi Kishimoto and his twin brother Seishi were born in 1974 in Okayama prefecture. They were born prematurely, and placed in an ICU immediately after birth. When he turned a year old, Kishimoto took part in a ceremony traditional in his village. During the ceremony, a rice cake is strapped to the back of the town's one-year old children, and three objects are placed in front of them. The child's future is divined by seeing which object he or she takes. His parents had chosen an abacus, a calligraphy brush and money as his three objects. His brother chose the brush, but Masashi went straight for the cash.

He began to take an interest in the things around him during his pre-school years (bugs and currents in rivers, for example). When something grabbed his attention, he had the habit of staring at it fixedly. His ability to concentrate while watching TV was apparently incredible. Even when his father called out "Hey! Mabo!" (Masashi's nickname), the boy's eyes would never waver from the television screen. His ability to concentrate, which has probably helped with his career as an author, was with him even as a child. Young Masashi particularly loved the Doraemon television anime series, and went through a phase of drawing nothing but Doraemon. If a friend presented him with an imperfect Doraemon sketch, Kishimoto would say, "that's not Doraemon, this is" and touch up the picture.

During elementary school, Kishimoto amused himself by doodling in his sketchbook. Even when he was in the middle of a game of hide-and-seek, he would trace Doraemon pictures on the ground to pass the time until he was found. Then, one day he saw an episode of Mobile Suit Gundam. Impressed by the series' graphics, he started drawing Mobile Suits in his notebook. He was also impressed by Akira Toriyama's Dr. Slump. He apparently developed a fascination with "visual styles."

During his last years of elementary school, the Dragonball anime was released, and this became the start of his love of the comic digest, Shonen Jump (published in the US by Viz). From television anime, he developed an interest in serialized manga and became obsessed with Dragonball. It seems that he even called series author Akira Toriyama his "god." So he churned out reproductions of the characters, apparently trying to appropriate the visual style of his god. Eventually, he began to seriously think about a career as a manga artist. The first manga he drew as a kid was called Hiatari-kun, and it was about a young Ninja.

In middle school, he joined his school's baseball club. At that time, a manga series called Touch was very popular. This manga seemed to mirror his own life as the main characters were twin brothers who played on their school's baseball team.

Kishimoto's drawing took a backseat to baseball. Games were played on weekends, and he had practice every morning. He also attended cram school, so unlike during his elementary school years, Masashi was really too busy to draw.

Just as he was starting to think he had outgrown doodling, he reached a major turning point. One day he saw a poster for the movie adaptation of Katsuhiro Otomo's Akira. Katsuhiro Otomo's artwork blew him away.

He became interested in manga again, hoping one day to be as good as Otomo, which even today is his stated goal as an artist. After his exposure to Akira, Kishimoto's ideas about art changed. He realized that originality was crucial. He studied various manga, but was really impressed only by the works of Toriyama and Otomo. As a result, Kishimoto tried to copy their artwork.

During college, he became aware of the importance of stories to manga, and began to study story writing. With the debut of Naruto, Kishimoto won the Hop Step Award for new artists, and his career as a manga artist was launched.

GLOSSARY(CAST)

A

Agari: Born in the Land of Waves. 48 yrs old. Female. The wife of Giichi, a colleague of Tazuna the bridge builder. She has no children of her own, so she dotes on Inari. Her hobby is knitting.

Ageha: Born in the Land of Waves. 7 yrs old. Female. An orphan whose parents were killed by Gato's gang. Although poor, she is bright, cheerful and lives life with a positive attitude.

Akado Manabu: A Ninja from the village of Konohagakure. 38 yrs old. Male. A veteran of the Chunin selection exams which he has taken 18 times. Has extensive knowledge but is weak and can't even get past the first part of the test.

Akado Yoroi: A Ninja from the village of Konohagakure. Male. Acts like a Ninja from Konohagakure, but is really a spy under orders from Orochimaru from village of Otogakure. Good at close combat, he has a technique in which he sucks out his opponent's Chakra rendering him or her unable to fight. He is also Kabuto's boss.

Akamaru: A Ninken (Ninja Dog) who is always at Kiba's side. Performs various combination techniques with his master. Bolsters weak-spirited Kiba during battle and galvanizes him into action.

Akame Iwana: A Ninja from the village of Konohagakure. 32 yrs old. Male. An elite, one-eyed Ninja. Lost his left eye during a spying mission in a foreign country. Searches for Naruto when he steals the Secret Manuscript from the third Lord Hokage's house.

Akane: The boss of the kids from the Land of Waves. 9 yrs old. Male. Tries to drown Inari and throws his dog in the sea. An unpleasant little bully.

Akimichi Choji: A Ninja from the village of Konohagakure. Genin. 13 yrs old. Male. Naruto's contemporary. Practices the secret arts of the Akimichi Clan which involve taking special power-up pills. He is very fond of eating and usually has something in his mouth. If he is called fat he gets really mad. Has been Shikamaru's best friend since childhood. When they work as a team they instinctively know what the other is thinking. Special skills include Baikajutsu and Nikudansensha. A compassionate soul, who would lay down his life for a friend.

Akimichi Choza: A Ninja from the village of Konohagakure. Jonin. 38 yrs old. Male. Choji's father. The good-natured head of the Akimichi Clan and pillar of the family. Part of the Inoshikacho Trio in his youth along with Inoichi and Shikaku. Takes great care in his son Choji's development and always watches over him indulgently. He knows that Choji has a kinder heart than anyone, and he himself is one of the kindest Ninja in the series.

Ami: A student at the Konohagakure Ninja Academy. 13 yrs old. Female. A classmate of

Sakura and Ino. Her grades are not too good. Likes to bully Sakura.

Anbu: The name of an organization in the village of Konohagakure. The official name is Ansatsu Senjutsu Tokushu Butai (lit. Assassination Tactics Special Division)'. Made up of the most skilled Ninja in the village, they hide their faces with animal masks. It is a position bestowed by Lord Hokage and their activities are not made public knowledge.

Asame: Born in the village of Konohagakure. 17 yrs old. Female. The daughter of Teuchi, owner of Naruto's favorite Ramen shop, Ichi Raku. Helps her father manage the business.

Azuma Shibito: A Jonin from the village of Iwagakure. 25 yrs old. Whilttled the Konoha defense unit down to just four surviving members with a devastating army. Soon afterwards, Killed by the Konoha no Kiiroi Senko (lit. Konoha's Yellow Flash), who later to becomes the fourth Lord Hokage.

B

Baiu: A Ninja from Amegakure. Age: 19. Male. Uses his small, agile body to get in close to his enemy for hand-to-hand combat. Although he is small, he is very powerful. Once he gets hold of his opponent he will hold them tight and crush them until they become lifeless.

Baki: A Ninja from Sunagakure. Jonin. Age: 30. Male. Under orders from Lord Kazekage he led Gaara and his team to the Chunin exams. Trusted implicitly by Lord Kazekage, he was sent partly to keep an eye on Gaara. A Ninja whose skills are rated highly in the village. He has a clear understanding of the unfavorable situation of the village (whose military strength has been weakened by the budget cuts from the feudal lord) and acts as an intermediary with Orochimaru's Otogakure village.

Bekko: A Ninja from Konohagakure. Chunin. Age: 41. Male. A veteran Ninja. Because he experienced the Fox Spirit incident first hand, he reacts with great distress at the news that Naruto has stolen the secret manuscript from Lord Hokage's house.

Buna: Apprentice Gardner. Age: 13. Male. When he sees Shimeji at work in the villages near Tanzaku Town, he is so impressed that he decides to become his apprentice. His ambition is to become a world-class gardener and works hard everyday to realize that goal.

C

Chohan: Gambler. Age: 33. Male. A regular customer at the gambling parlors. Plays a game with Jiraiya, using information on Tsunade as his wager. He loses the bet due to Naruto's interference.

Choseki: Missing-Nin. Age: 27. Male. Hides behind Gantetsu's notoriety and does as he pleases. Commits crimes ranging from extortion to blackmail wherever he goes.

D

Daichi: A student at the Konohagakure Ninja Academy. Age: 10. Male. The child with the dazzling smile. He has a smart mouth, but deep down is very kind. When asked: "What is important to you?" by the third Hokage, he simply replies "friends."

Dan: A Ninja from Konohagakure. Jonin. Male. A Ninja who was active during the Ninja Wars. He loses his beloved sister, but risks his life to protect the village without despairing. Dan was Tsunade's lover in her younger days.

Danzo: A Ninja from Konohagakure. Genin. Age: 18. Male. During the Chunin exam, he makes it to the Forest of Death, only to be disqualified along with Shibire and Mireji when they decide to open their scroll.

Dengaku: Owns an Oden restaurant in the Post Station Town. Age: 33. Male. Owner of an Oden (a Japanese dish consisting of hard-boiled eggs, Japanese white radish, fish-paste, and other filler boiled in broth) restaurant that Tsunade and Jiraiya visit. His Oden is apparently very addictive, especially when accompanied by alcohol.

Doki: Three demons summoned using Kuchiyose by Tayuya, a member of the Oto no Yoninshu. Their actions are completely controlled by Tayuya's whistle. They each use their own signature attacks – one has a huge club, another has a weird, backward-facing posture – to send their enemies into the abyss.

Dosu Kinuta: A Ninja from Otogakure. Age: 14. Male. One of three people who participate in the Chunin exam as Orochimaru's spies. His appearance is strange indeed, and his facial expressions are impossible to read due to the gauze wrapped around his head. He is very aggressive, and specializes in attacks that disorient his opponent with sound. However, if the battle does not go his way, he is not above begging for mercy.

E

Ebisu: A Ninja from Konohagakure. Age: 28. Special Jonin. Male. An elite private teacher who likes to boast that has prepared many prospective candidates for the role of Lord Hokage. Teaches the grandson of the third Lord Hokage, Konohamaru, and also trains Naruto in Chakra-control.

Emi: The staff of a first-class haberdashery in the Post Station Town. Age: 25. Female. A beautiful girl that has even Jiraiya gog-eyed. When she goes to visit her friend in the pleasure district she is kidnapped by Itachi.

Enko-o Enma: The monkey spirit that the third Lord Hokage has signed a pact with in his blood and summons by Kuchiyose. Can turn his own body into a weapon in the form of a telescopic staff called Kongobo (a reference to the TV program "Monkey Magic"?), and is a veteran soldier. He is always at the third Lord Hokage's side on the battlefield.

F

Feudal Lord of the Land of Wind: The ruler of the Land of Wind, which is situated to the South-West of the Land of Fire. He feared seriously weakening his country through a long war, so he made a treaty with the countries around him to bring about peace. He took this opportunity to reduce the budget given to the village of Sunagakure which controls the military force.

Fuki: A student at the Konohagakure Ninja Academy. Age: 13. Female. Likes to be fashionable and is particularly fond of makeup. During the days at the academy she ganged up with Ami and Kasumi and bullied Sakura.

Funeno Daikoku: A Ninja from Konohagakure. Chunin. Age: 36. Male. He was a teacher at the Ninja Academy who taught Itachi. When he encounters Itachi, he says that he has never seen such a superb student

Futaba: A student at the Konohagakure Ninja Academy. Age: 9. Female. A slightly weak-willed, but kind-hearted girl. When Lord Hokage asks the students, "Who are the most important people in your lives?", she replies that the most important people to her are her parents, older brother and dog.

G

Gaara: A Ninja from Sunagakure. Age: 12. Male. His father is Lord Kazekage. Before he was born he had the Shukaku spirit embedded in his body. Performed incredible feats at the Chunin exam in Konohagakure, which made him the focus of everyone's attention. Uses techniques involving sand which he keeps in the big gourd he carries around on his back. Sometimes the Shukaku spirit in his body takes over and he is unable to control his own actions.

Gama: A giant frog that Jiraiya made a pact with signed in his own blood. Whenever he is summoned he appears immediately by Jiraiya's side ready for action.

Gamabunta: Naruto summons Gamabunta by Kuchiyose during one of the Jutsu challenges that Jiraiya gives him. He is an enormous and incredibly powerful giant frog. Because his power is greater than those who summon him, he has an arrogant attitude and doesn't care much what other people think. It is not surprising given his enormous power and size.

Gama Kich: Gamabunta's eldest son. A frog with a small body. Because he is still a child he hasn't had any opportunities to serve in battle, but judging by his tough-talking father, we can see what kind of a future he has in store. He looks forward to the day when he is big enough to fight.

Gamatatsu: Gamabunta's second son. Unlike his brother Gama Kishi, he is lazy and spoiled. He is always thinking about snacks.

Gantetsu: A Ninja who makes regular appearances at the Post Station Town and boasts that he is a super-powerful Densetsu no Yaminin (lit. Legendary Dark Ninja). Age: 29. Male. Took on Jiraiya, but was easily defeated.

Gato: Runs a merchant shipping company

called Gato Company, which is a front for his illegal operations. He uses Ninja as muscle in order to sell drugs, take over companies and terrorize whole countries. Through economic and military means, he kept a tight grip on the Land of Waves' transport access and tried to stop Tazuna building a bridge to the mainland. A ruthless man who will stop at nothing to get his way.

Gekkou Hayate: A Ninja from Konohagakure. Tokubetsu (Special) Jonin. Age: 23. Male. Appears as a judge for the preliminary round of the third phase of the Chunin exams. Seems to be constantly sick, which makes him stand out among the generally healthy Ninja in the village of Konohagakure. He is selected as a judge for the Chunin exams because of his level-headed, calm nature and sound judgment. Never once losing his cool, he is forced on numerous occasions to step in and stop the fights from going too far.

Gennai: A Ninja from Konohagakure. Genin. Male. An examinee in the Chunin exams. Was disqualified because teammate Komugi dropped out before the tenth question in the first part of the exam.

Genyumaru: The current body playing host to Orochimaru's soul. In a hurry to select a new host body and in the absence of Sasuke, Orochimaru decides to select his next victim by locking a big group of Ninja in a cave together and making them fight till there is only one man standing. That person is Genyumaru. Unfortunately for him, his outstanding fighting skills means he ends up becoming Orochimaru's next host.

Genzo: A resident of Konohagakure. Age: 58. Male. Photographer. The number one photographer in the village, he has been in charge of the photos in the Ninja yearbook for many years.

Giichi: A resident of the Land of Waves. Age: 49. Male. A bridge builder who was working together with Tazuna. He temporarily gave up building the bridge under pressure from Gato's men, but touched by Inari's courage, rose up against them.

Goshiki: A resident of Tanzaku Town. Age: 37. Male. A guide at the Tanzaku Castle. When the castle is destroyed by Orochimaru and he panics and runs away. Naruto and Jiraiya happen to be passing, so he informs them of the situation.

Genzo: A resident of Tanzaku Town. Age: 37. Male. A guide at the Tanzaku Castle. When the castle is destroyed by Orochimaru and he panics and runs away. Naruto and Jiraiya happen to be passing, so he informs them of the situation.

H

Hagane Kotetsu: A Ninja from Konohagakure. Chunin. Age: 24. Male. Often works together with Izumo selecting Ninja with the appropriate talents to become Chunin. Sometimes uses rather heavy-handed methods to test those Ninja's abilities.

Haimaru San Kyodai (Three Haimaru Brothers): The three Ninja Dogs which work with Inuzukai Hana (Kiba's older sister). Normally gentle and quiet, when they get into battle they attack the enemy with great fighting spirit.

Haku: A Ninja from Kirigakure. Age: 15. Male. A loyal and devoted right-hand man to Zabuza, with remarkable skills. He possesses the same hereditary Sharingan as members of the Uchiha Clan. Normally wears a mask, but his face, when revealed, is so beautiful that he is easily mistaken for a girl. He attacks Naruto and his team when they are on a mission to protect Tazuna the bridge builder, but because of his inherently good character, he is unable to bring himself to kill them. He loses the fight and dies alongside Zabuza.

Haruno Sakura: A Ninja from Konohagakure. Genin. Age: 13. Female. Part of a team with Sasuke and Naruto. At the beginning she doesn't seem to have much to contribute as a Ninja, but she has an incredible memory, excellent Chakra control, and is highly skilled at Genjutsu. Kakashi rates her highly. After she meets Tsunade, she realizes her calling as a Medical Ninja and, working as Tsunade's assistant, rapidly begins acquiring healing skills. Sasuke is her first and only love.

Hatake Kakashi: A Ninja from Konohagakure. Jonin. Age: 26. Male. The leader of Naruto's team. An easy-going character who rarely shows his emotions and never loses his cool. Known throughout the Five Great Countries as the "Copy" Ninja (on account of his Sharingan), he is one of Konohagakure's strongest Jonin. Using the eye that his best friend Obito gave him before he died, he is able to size up the strength of an opponent, analyze their state of mind from the way they are breathing and

their general demeanor, and even predict what their next move will be. In addition, he is able to analyze an opponent's move as they are performing it, and copy it perfectly himself, all within a split second (hence the nickname). He has learnt more than 1000 techniques this way. An excellent teacher, Sasuke, Naruto and Sakura's remarkable progress owes a lot to his methods of instruction.

Hayase: A Ninja from Konohagakure. Chunin. Age: 24. Male. Devised the questions for the first part of the Chunin exams. A very sharp-minded character.

Hibari: A student at the Konohagakure Ninja Academy. Age: 9. Female. A star Kunoichi (female Ninja) student in the same year as Konohamaru. She gets good marks and is a favorite of Iruka's.

Hijiri Shimon: A Ninja from Konohagakure. Chunin. Age: 26. Male. Invigilated during the first part of the Chunin exams. With his skilled eye, he is able to detect cheating and disqualifies one examinee after another.

Hokage (the first): A Ninja from Konohagakure. The founder of the village of Konohagakure. A master of the Katon Jutsu as well as inventor of the Mokuton Jutsu, he was a highly skilled Ninja, whose remarkable exploits are talked about even to this day. He thought of the villagers as part of his own body, and kept constant vigil over Konohagakure. He established the concept of protecting the village as a founding principle, which the Ninja of Konoha still maintain as their most fundamental value.

Hokage (the second): A Ninja from Konohagakure. He was the younger brother of the first Lord Hokage, and acceded to the position after his predecessor's death. In contrast to his easy-going brother, he had a passionate, determined character. He was a strict leader who put efforts into establishing the organizations and systems of power in the village. The fact that Konohagakure has such a strong administrative system in comparison to Shinobi villages in other countries is largely due to him.

Hokage (the third): A Ninja from Konohagakure. A favorite student of the first Lord Hokage who put great effort into further developing the village that his two predecessors had built up. He is an ardent exponent of the values established by the founding Hokage (of protecting the village), and is always lecturing the young Ninja in the village on the importance of upholding them. Nicknamed the "Professor", he is a specialist researcher of techniques who knows (and can use) every Jutsu that has ever been invented in the village. Is later killed by Orochimaru.

Hokage (the fourth): A Ninja of Konohagakure. Prizing the safety of the village above all else, he took on the Nine-Tailed Fox Spirit that was threatening to destroy Konohagakure and sealed it inside the body of the newly born Naruto using a technique which he knew would result in his own death. He placed great importance on team work during his tenure as Hokage, and taught these values to young Ninja such as Kakashi. He was known far and wide by the alias Kiiroi Senko (lit. Bright Yellow Flash), because of the extreme speed with which he would attack on the battlefield.

Hoki: A Ninja from Takigakure. Genin. Age: 17. Male. He is one of the six examinees from the village of Takigakure who take part in the Chunin exams. Did well getting through the first part of the exam, but ran out of steam in the Forest of Death.

Hosei: A Ninja from Konohagakure. Genin. Age: 18. Male. Took part in the Chunin exams, but dropped out before the tenth question in the first part of the exam.

Hoshigaki Kisame: A Ninja from Kirigakure. Age: 29. Male. A deserter from the village of Kirigakure, he is classified as an S Rank criminal (the highest ranking) for the suspected part he has played in various subversive acts, including the assassination of a feudal lord. A member of the secret Akatsuki organization, he takes his orders from Uchiha Itachi. Carries a big sword around with him which he calls Samehada (lit. Sharkskin).

Hosho: A Ninja from Konohagakure. Medical Team. Age: 26. Male. Took part in the rescue mission of Shikamaru and his team, who had been sent to get back Sasuke from the Oto no Yoninshu (Sound 4). A very kind-hearted Ninja.

Hyuga Hanabi: A student at the Konohagakure Ninja Academy. Age: 8. Female. Hinata's younger sister, she is by far the more gifted of the two, and was given special education by her father Hiashi. However, because she is still young, she has no practical fighting experience and her talents remain an unknown quantity.

Hyuga Hiashi: A Ninja from Konohagakure. Age: 42. Male. The head of the Hyuga Clan, one of the strongest of the Konohagakure families. Having decided that his eldest daughter Hinata had no talent, he gave up on her and personally trained her younger sister Hanabi, of whom he has great expectations. He has a tendency to be hard-hearted when it comes to the prestige of the clan.

Hyuga Hinata: A Ninja from Konohagakure. Genin. Age: 13. Female. Because she is born as the heir to the main branch of the Hyuga Clan, there is a lot of pressure on her to live up to expectations. She is a shy, retiring girl and, regardless of whether she has talent or not, she makes little progress and seems likely to buckle under this pressure. However, after she hears words of encouragement from Naruto during the Chunin exam, she overcomes her fear and starts to make rapid progress acquiring Ninja skills.

Hyuga Hizashi: A Ninja from Konohagakure. Male. He is born as the younger twin brother of Hiashi, and is demoted to the branch family as a result. Observing the strict code that the branch family is bound by, he acts as Hiashi's body-double in order to protect him and is killed in the process.

Hyuga Neji: A Ninja from Konohagakure. Genin. Age: 14. Male. Born from the noble Hyuga family, and considered the most talented Ninja in his clan. However, because he is a member of a branch family he must abide by the code of the clan and pledge his allegiance to serve the main family, which he thoroughly resents. Naruto convinces him that fate does not control his destiny and that he can chose his own path. Once he hears these words, his whole outlook on life begins to change. He possesses the Byakugan (hereditary ability of the Hyuga family), with which he is able to see through his opponent's body and which allows him to target his opponent's nervous system. He uses this in combination with a technique called Juken which inflicts damage on his opponent's internal organs

I

Ibara: A resident of Konohagakure. Female. She knows that the Nine-Tailed Fox Spirit is sealed inside Naruto, and after he fails the Ninja Academy graduation exam, says a mean thing to him.

Inaho: A Kunoichi (female Ninja) from Konohagakure. Genin. In the same cell as Komugi and Gennai. Disqualified from the Chunin selection exam because her teammate Komugi gave up halfway through.

Inari: A resident the Land of Waves. Male. The son-in-law of Saiza, who is said to be a hero of the Land of Waves. He was living in despair because Saiza was killed by Gato, but after he meets Naruto his courage and hope returns.

Inuzuka Hana: A Ninja from Konohagakure. Chunin. Age: 18. Female.

Kiba's sister. She keeps three Ninja dogs called Haimaru San Kyodai (lit. Three Haimaru Brothers). The complete opposite of her mother and younger brother, she is calm and collected. She is also an excellent vet.

Inuzuka Kiba: A Ninja from Konohagakure. Genin. Age: 13. Male. A member of the Inuzuka Clan. Researches techniques which involve his Ninken (Ninja Dog) Akamaru. Since Akamaru was born they have always been by each other's side and have a bond closer than brothers. During battle, Kiba and Akamaru attack together using sophisticated combination techniques. Skilled at Jujin Bunshin Jutsu (Half-Best Clone), Giju Ninpo (lit. Beast Imitation Ninja Technique) and various other forms of attack. Has a super-enhanced sense of smell.

Inuzuka Tsume: A Ninja from Konohagakure. Jonin. Age: 38. Female. Kiba's mother. During the attempted coup d'etat by Orochimaru, Tsume and Kuromaru (her beloved Ninja Dog) are the first to take on the enemy. She is courageous, but has an impulsive and tempestuous character.

Iyashi: A Ninja from Konohagakure. Male. A junior member of a medical team. Was on standby during the Chunin selection exams in case of injury.

J

Janto: Gambler. Age: 52. Male. A shrewd and proficient gambler who drifts between the gambling hubs of various areas, he enjoys a good game. However, he's not very in the loop, as he is unaware that Tsunade is rumored to be a "Sitting Duck" among the gambling community.

Jimei: A Ninja from Konohagakure. Genin. Age: 16. Male. During the first of the Chunin selection trials, he is disqualified for cheating. He wasn't quite skilled enough to slip past the exam officials.

Jiraiya: A Ninja from Konohagakure. Age: 50. Male. Jiraiya, along with Orochimaru and Tsunade are known as the Legendary Three Ninja of Konohagakure. Using Kuchiyose, he can summon the enormous toad, Gamabunta that can crush virtually any foe with his overwhelming power. Jiraiya also travels the country under the alias Toad Hermit looking for ideas for his novels, and is the author of Make-out Paradise, of which Kakashi is an avid fan. When Naruto inherits the role of trainer from Kakashi, Jiraiya initiates him into Kuchiyose techniques and the Rasengan (Spiraling Sphere) technique.

Jirobo: A member of the Oto no Yoninshu (Sound 4). Age: 14. Male. Built like a sumo wrestler, Jirobo mows down his enemies with sheer strength. He consumes his opponent's Chakra, turning it into his own energy. Although he seems to have a violent temper, and often tries to incite his opponents, Jirobo in fact uses this as a strategy to make them lose their cool; he can actually be quite crafty, and is able to make calm tactical assessments.

K

Kagari: A Ninja from Otogakure. Genin. Age: 17. Male. He is in a team with Oboro and Mubi. Together they attack using three-man combination moves. His main role in the team is to keep look out. Normally he is blindfolded, but this is so that he can be more keenly aware of approaching Ninja using his other senses. He is an unassuming character, but when the team work together using Genjutsu as their main form of attack, having the edge that Kagari's skill affords is an invaluable asset.

Kaiza: A resident of the Land of Waves. Male. A hot-blooded character who has come from overseas to the Land of Waves in search of fame and fortune. He is proactive and has great natural courage. Hailed as hero by the people of the Land of Waves. He looks after Inari as if he were his own son, but is murdered by Gato (who plans to conquer the Land of Waves) because he stands up to him.

Kaji: A resident of the Land of Waves. Works as a boatman. Age: 39. Male. The captain of a boat which has been taking people from the Land of Waves to other countries for 20 years. He knows all the sea routes around the island and can switch courses whenever the situation demands it.

Kakko: A Ninja from Iwagakure. Jonin. One of the best Ninja from this village – a master of Genjutsu, Taijutsu and Ninjutsu. With plenty of battle experience, he later kills Uchiwa Obito but is then put in a tight spot by the young Kakashi.

Kamatari: A one-eyed weasel that Temari summons by Kuchiyose. His movements are very quick and he attacks by riding on the wind that Temari creates with her giant fan. He brandishes a sickle which is heavier than his own body weight and can use it to flatten everything or one around him.

Kamizuki Izumo: A Ninja from Konohagakure. Chunin. Age: 24. Male. A judge for the Chunin exams, he is fairly cool towards the examinees. Occasionally when he is talking about the young Genin, however, there is a tone in his voice which betrays the interest he takes in their education and the older-brotherly feeling he has for them.

Kankuro: A Ninja from Sunagakure. Genin. Age: 14. Male. Gaara's older brother. Usually carries one or two strange puppets around with him, which sometimes act like his clone. He likes to fight. Even if his opponent is unarmed, he has no problems hurting them.

Kanpo: A Ninja from Konohagakure. Age: 27. Female. Leader of a medical team. She was the leader of the medical team on stand-by at the test site of the third part of the Chunin exam. She nursed Neji after his fight with Naruto.

Kaori: A resident of Konohagakure. Age: 28. Female. She is in charge of Lee after he sustains a serious injury in his fight against Gaara. She has her hands full with Lee, who generally makes a racket and keeps trying to carry on training, but she looks after him kindly.

Karura: A Ninja from Sunagakure. Female. When she is pregnant with Lord

Kazekage's baby, she has the Shukaku spirit embedded in her and dies while giving birth to Gaara. She didn't want to give birth to Gaara, because she knew she would have to sacrifice her life in the process. She died cursing the village for her fate.

Kashike: A student at the Sunagakure Ninja Academy. Male. Was a classmate of Gaara when he was little. After a fight with Gaara in which he gets hurt, Gaara brings him some medicine as a peace-offering, but Kashike turns him down. Even now he is scared of Gaara. An edgy character from the start, if someone comes to his house, he only opens the door a small crack.

Kasumi: A student at the Konohagakure Ninja Academy. Age: 13. Female. Bullied Sakura with Ami.

Katsuyu: A giant slug which Tsunade summons by Kuchiyose. Has a polite manner and compliant nature, give quite a quiet impression. However, his skills are an equal match for Gamabunta and Manda in battle.

Kazabune: A resident of the Post Station Town and balloon-stall owner. Age: 41. Male. Sells water balloons on a float during festivals. Normally wanders from town to town selling kids toys making a livelihood as a traveling salesman.

Kazekage: Leader of Sunagakure. Male. One of the five ruling Lords. Worrying about the strength of the village after the feudal lord of the Land of Wind cuts the village's budget, he turns his own son Gaara into an unnaturally strong Ninja. Later assassinated by Orochimaru.

Kidomaru: A member of the Oto no Yoninshu (Sound 4). Age: 14. Male. Can skillfully manipulate threads of Chakra in complicated patterns using his six arms during battle. Of the four in the group he is the most dexterous and technically skilled. Even in the highly charged context of a fight, he is able to make up his own rules and enjoy the fight as though it were a game.

Kin Tsuchi: A Ninja from Otogakure. Age: 14. Female. The only Kunoichi (female Ninja) from the village of Otogakure to take part in the Chunin selection exams. She has a cold-hearted, jealous nature and is envious of Sakura's beautiful hair. In the preliminary heats before the third part of the exam she employs a high speed form of attack, using Senbon (throwing needles) with bells attached to them, but goes out to quick-thinking Shikamaru.

Kito: A Ninja from Konohagakure. Age: 27. Male. Medical team. Along with Shizune treated the badly wounded Neji after the Chunin exam. A healing specialist with exceptional Chakra control which he can sustain for over three hours.

Kohada: A resident of Konohagakure. Age: 19. Female. The daughter of a Sushi shop owner. Jiraiya spies on her while she is bathing at the public baths. She does all the housework while helping out at the Sushi shop. She is good-natured and well-liked by all the regular customers.

Koji: A student at the Konohagakure Ninja Academy. Male. He is a class joker in the same year as Konohamaru. Although he is set on becoming the fifth Lord Hokage, his grades are not so hot.

Komaza: A Ninja from Sunagakure. Genin. Age: 16. Male. During the first part of the Chunin exams he is caught cheating and is disqualified.

Komugi: A Ninja from Konohagakure. Genin. Sits next to Naruto in the first part of the Chunin exams. He is the team leader but drops out of the exam before the tenth question

Kota: A student at the Konohagakure Ninja Academy. Age: 13. Male. In the same year as Sasuke and Shikamaru. Has a great deal of curiosity and will poke his nose into anyone's business. When he notices the family insignia of the Uchiha clan on Sasuke's back he starts to develop an interest in him.

Kumo no Kuni (Land of Clouds) no Shinobi Gashira: A Ninja from the village of Kumogakure. An ambassador sent with the official purpose of brokering a peace deal between the villages of Konohagakure and Kumogakure which had been at war for some time. The real, hidden purpose of his visit is to kidnap Hyuga Hinata, heir to the main branch of the Hyuga Clan, in order to learn the secret of the Byakugan (White Eye), a Kekkeigenkai ability unique to that clan. The kidnap fails and he is killed by Hyuga Hiashi.

Kuromaru: A one-eyed Ninken (Ninja Dog) who fights alongside Inuzukai Tsume and has had much battle experience. He is old but has lost none of his strength.

Kusabi: One of Gato's gang. Age: 23. Male. One of the gangsters hired by Gato. He runs away when Gato gets killed and the people of the Land of Waves rise up against his gang.

Kusuma: Works at a mask shop in the Post Station Town. Age: 29. Male. Loves children and goes from town to town selling masks. He tells Naruto off for walking around with a mask on.

Kusushi: A Ninja from Konohagakure. Age: 24. Male. Medical Team. He is ordered by the fifth Lord Hokage to try and find Sasuke's rescue team. On the way he meets Kakashi, learns from him that the team is safe and returns to the village to pass on the news.

M

Might Guy: A Ninja from Konohagakure. Jonin. Age: 27. Male. A Taijutsu specialist who has trained his body to the peak of physical perfection. Teaches his many well-honed Taijutsu techniques to Rock Lee and his team. He thinks of Kakashi as his rival and is always striving to outdo him.

Mitarashi Anko: A Ninja from Konohagakure. Tokubetsu Jonin. Age: 25. Female. She is in charge of the second part of the Chunin exams. Her character and facial expression are normally bright and cheerful, but every now and again she appears troubled by something. This can perhaps be accounted for by the fact that Orochimaru was formerly her teacher. Now she does what she can to prevent Orochimaru from realizing his ambitions. She likes sweet things.

Mitokado Homura: A member of the Konohagakure Goikenban (Advisory Council). Age: 69. Male. The purpose of the Goikenban is to provide support to Lord Hokage, constantly assess the changing circumstances, and advise him on the correct policy direction for the village. Homura is a veteran member of the council and has been active since the third Lord Hokage's first term.

Mizuki: A Ninja from Konohagakure. Chunin. Age: 27. Male. In charge of the teachers at the Ninja Academy. Has a kind face and gives the impression of being very gentle and considerate. However, this is just a front he puts on. In fact he is an ambitious Ninja who strives to acquire power by fair means or foul. Encourages Naruto to steal the secret manuscript from the third Lord Hokage's house so he can get it for himself. His plan fails, and he gets killed.

Momochi Zabuza: A Ninja originally from Kirigakure. Age: 26. Male. His enormous sword and ruthless personality have earned him the nickname Kirigakure no Kijin (lit. Demon Man of Kirigakure). Formerly the Kirigakure Ninja Academy's graduation exam took the form of a fight to the death among the students in the year. Zabuza is infamous for killing a hundred students during his graduation exam. A member of the village Anbu, his deadly Silent Killing technique made him a very effective assassin. Staged a coup d'etat in the village which failed. He then left the village. Appears during Naruto's first assignment to the Land of Waves and tries to stop the team from completing the mission.

N

Namiashi Raido: A Ninja from Konohagakure. Tokubetsu Jonin. Age: 32. Male. A young elite who enjoyed the complete confidence of the third Hokage. A very strong-hearted man, he never gives up in the face of adversity.

Nara Shikaku: A Ninja from Konohagakure. Jonin. Age: 38. Male. Nara Shikamaru's father. He always remains calm, and does not panic even when in physical danger. His personal philosophy is "the way of the Ninja is faith," and he passed his words and convictions on to Shikamaru.

Nara Shikamaru: A Ninja from Konohagakure. Chunin. Age: 13. Male. Of the Ninja in Naruto's year, he was the first to be given the Chunin rank. He was not very active in his role as a Ninja, preferring to "be a casual Ninja, a casual worker, and live a normal life." However, his abilities as a strategist are highly rated – he is able to clearly assess situations and appropriately decide his next move – resulting in his selection for Chunin rank. He becomes more actively engaged in his work on becoming a Chunin. His signature Ninjustu is the Kagemane no Jutsu (Shadow Imitation Technique), which is a relatively simple technique, but because Shikanomaru has mastered its use, any opponent that gets hit with it will have a rough time.

Nara Yoshino: A Ninja from Konohagakure. Chunin. Age: 36. Female. Shikamaru's mother. She's strict with her son, even stricter with her husband. Never one to offer soothing words, Yoshino puts her boot to her husband and son's backsides to motivate them. Of course, she does this out of love for her family.

Nawaki: A Ninja from Konohagakure. Genin. Male. Grandson of the first Hokage and Tsunade's younger brother. Idolizes his grandfather, and trains to become a strong Ninja so that he too may one day wear the title of Hokage. Loses his life during the Ninja Wars.

Nejiri: A Ninja from Sunagakure. Genin. Age: 16. Male. During the first Chunin exam, he sits next to Sakura.

Ninkame: The huge turtle with whom Guy has a Kuchiyose contract. It is a magnificent creature, and Lee probably respects its words as much as those of Guy, his teacher.

Nine-tailed Fox Spirit: A legendary spirit who almost wiped out the village of Konohagakure in just one day. The fourth Lord Hokage sacrificed his own life and imprisoned the spirit in the newly-born Naruto in order to save the village. The fox spirit did not die in the process and continues to exert its influence on Naruto from within his body. Sometimes it releases great amounts of Chakra that Naruto can use. At those times Naruto displays an unnatural power.

Nobori: A student at the Konohagakure Ninja Academy. Age: 10. Male. Classmate of Konohamaru. He is good friends with Daichi, and the two are always together though sometimes they quarrel.

O

Oboro: A Ninja from Amegakure. Genin. Age: 17. Male. He works together with team-mates Kagari and Mubi to perform three-man coordinated attacks. In the Shi no Mori (Forest of Death) he uses Genjutsu to create multiple phantom opponents in a fight with Naruto and his team.

Okei: A Ninja from Konohagakure. Chunin. Age: 23. Male. During the Chunin selection exam he disguises himself as an examinee and tries to encourage other examinees to cheat.

Okyo: A resident of Konohagakure. Age: 19. Female. The poster girl for the Masugame izakaya (bar). Jiraiya spies on her while she is playing in the river near the baths before work.

Oni Kyodai: Ninja born in the village of Kirigakure. Male. Gato hires them to assassinate Tazuna, the bridge builder. Because of their bond of blood, they can synchronize their attacks with consummate skill. Their special weapon is a retractable razor chain which has a kind of metal glove with knife-like claws at either end. Each brother takes one glove and they use the chain to slice their opponents in two, creating a shower of blood.

Orochimaru: One of the Legendary Three Ninja of the village of Konohagakure. Age: 50. Male. A genius who has turned to the dark side, he harbors evil ambitions and researches the forbidden art of immortality. When his research is discovered, his route to becoming Lord Hokage is blocked and he leaves the village to establish his own village, Otogakure. Uses the opportunity of the Chunin exams to stage a coup against the village of Konohagakure. The plan fails but in the process he murders the third Lord

Hokage. He continues to act suspiciously.

Otokaze: A Ninja from Sunagakure. Jonin. Age: 26. Male. Always on look-out, whenever there's a situation he blows a whistle to warn his friends. His main duties are keeping look-out and passing on messages. The first to discover Kazekage's body after he has been killed by Orochimaru. He is known for being an ardent whistle collector.

Otoha: A resident of Konohagakure. Age: 21. Female. A nurse employed at the Konoha hospital. Enjoys relaxing after work at the public baths. She is too busy with work to have a boyfriend.

Otora: A resident of Sunagakure. Unemployed. Age: 49. Male. An unfortunate guy who is killed by Gaara when he accidentally bumps into him while walking along drunk. An alcoholic to the end, even when he dies his hand is still clutching the bottle.

P

Pakkun: A Ninja Dog that Kakashi summons by Kuchiyose. A specialist in using Ninja Dogs, Kakashi has a particular affection for Pakkun.

Pochi: The pet dog of Inari (a boy from the Land of Waves).

R

Rin: A Ninja from Konohagakure. Chunin. Female. Fought in the Battle of Kannabi Bridge with Kakashi and Obito, but was taken captive. A master of healing techniques, she has a warm and gentle nature. If one of her colleagues gets injured she gets straight down to business.

Rock Lee: A Ninja from Konohagakure. Genin. Age: 14. Male. He is completely unable to perform Genjutsu or Ninjutsu, but is unnaturally skilled at Taijutsu as a result of pure hard work on his part. He adores his teacher Guy, and strives continuously to master ever more difficult Taijutsu techniques. His name and facial features are said to be based on the movie star, Bruce Lee.

S

Sajin : A Ninja from Sunagakure. Chunin. Age: 23. Male. Sunagakure Ninja who participates in the coup d'etat staged by Orochimaru. He is caught by Nara Shikaku's Kage Shibari no Jutsu, and finished off by the Kage Kubi Shibari no Jutsu. A fairly green Chunin, with little experience under his belt.

Sakon Ukon: A member of the Oto no Yoninshu (Sound 4). Age: 14. Male. Twin brothers who can merge their cells, forming a single, shared body. Because they share a single body, they can operate 24 hours a day – while one twin is awake, the other sleeps to restore his Chakra. Although they share a single body, the brothers have different personalities, which allow them to each other objectively. They serve as the leader of the Oto no Yoninshu and keep the other three organized.

Sarugaku Tsuzumi: A Ninja from Konohagakure. Chunin. Age: 25. Male. In charge of security during the third part of the Chunin exam.

Sarutobi Asuma: A Ninja from Konohagakure. Jonin. Age: 27. Male. Asuma doesn't seem very Ninja-like, as he's always shown calmly smoking. This belies the fact that he is one of Konohagakure's foremost Ninja, with abilities approaching those of Kakashi. This fact is demonstrated when he easily wipes out eight Oto Ninja that attack Shikamaru. In training his three underlings, Shikamaru, Choji and Ino, he takes a hands-off approach that encourages them to be independent.

Satetsu: A Ninja from Sunagakure. Jonin. Age: 28. Male. Sunagakure Ninja who participates in the coup d'etat staged by Orochimaru, and afterwards tries to track down the missing Kazekage. He rushes to the scene when news of Lord Kazekage's death reaches him, and is dismayed upon identifying the body.

Shiba: A Ninja from Kusagakure. Chunin. Age: 20. Male. Powerful warrior from Kusagakure Village. During the Chunin exam, some feudal lords attempt to rig Shiba's match for gambling purposes, but he's killed by Gaara anyway.

Shibire: A Ninja from Konohagakure. Genin. Age: 19. Male. Shibire belongs to the same group as Tanzo and Minoji. Pressed for time during the Chunin exam, he opens his scroll, and is knocked out by the exam official who appears, resulting in his disqualification from the exam.

Shigure: A Ninja from Amegakure. Age: 19. Male. An elite warrior sent to the Konohagakure Village Chunin exam by the Amegakure Village authorities. Meets Gaara's group just after the start of the second exam, and uses the Joro Senbon technique to drive them back, but faced with a superior foe he is defeated along with his friends.

Shimeji: Gardener. Age: 57. Male. A resourceful gardener who makes his living working various villages and towns around Tanzaku. A touch from his hand will immediately restore even the most neglected of gardens.

Shinta: A resident of Konohagakure. Age: 14. Male. When Shinta was about four, he used to play with Choji, but being a bully, he left Choji out of his Ninja games and teased him. He is self-centered, and speaks without considering what others will think of him.

Shiranui Genma : A Ninja from Konohagakure. Tokubetsu Jonin. Age: 29. Male. Worked as an examiner of the Chunin exam. A man of great talent, he is often called on to perform other difficult jobs. Although normally light-hearted, he never panics in tight spots, and deals with situations calmly.

Shizune: A Ninja from Konohagakure. Jonin. Age: 28. Female. Apprentice and partner to Tsunade. Her skill with medical techniques is exceptional. Although Tsunade can be very demanding at times, Shizune serves her with unfailing dedication and love, placing top priority on her mentor's physical well-being.

Shu: Cat. Age: 3. Lives in Tanzaku. Watching this cat play gives Naruto the hint that allows him to obtain the Rasengan (Spiraling Sphere) technique.

Shukaku: The spirit of an old monk, in the form of a Tanuki (raccoon-dog) that was sealed in a tea-kettle. He was transferred to Gaara's fetus, and now comprises part of Gaara's body and psyche. He can take on his true form by using the Tanuki Neiri (Tanuki Sleep) technique to put Gaara to sleep and taking full control of his body.

Sozu: Gambler. Age: 36. Male. Regular customer at the Tanzaku gambling houses, where he has the highest betting average. He fleeces Tsunade for a considerable sum, and then goes drinking in the town.

Sukima: A Ninja from Konohagakure. Genin. Age: 17. Male. Takes the Chunin selection exam. Only lasts 25 minutes in the first exam. He is the first to be disqualified due to excessive cheating.

Sumashi: A Ninja from Iwagakure. Tokubetsu Jonin. Age: 26. Male. During the Ninja Wars, he attacked Kakashi's group, which had advanced to his position inside his ally's territory. The Doton: Retsudotensho technique he performs cooperatively with his teammates is powerful enough to open up fissures in the ground.

Susuki: Resident of the Post Station Town. Age: 21. Female. A night hostess, she keeps Jiraiya entertained. She has a rivalry with coworker Momiji, and the two are always competing for popularity. Her weapons are her gorgeous hair and smile

Suzume: A Ninja from Konohagakure. Chunin. Age: 31. Female. Suzume was in charge of classes at Ninja Academy when Sakura was a kid. In addition to being an accomplished Ninja, she is also generally knowledgeable in flower arranging, handi-

crafts, and tea ceremony. She is a famous instructor, who is both firm and kind. Her teaching philosophy is "clarity, justness, and beauty."

T

Taiseki: A Ninja from Iwagakure. Male. He has a very cool character. He always carries out his tasks competently. He can hide using a camouflage technique, then attack opponents from their blind side, dealing a single, fatal blow. Together with Kakko, he pulls off an exquisite feint, and manages to capture Rin, who is Kakashi's ally.

Tatami Iwashi: A Ninja from Konohagakure. Chunin. Age: 23. Male. During the Chunin exams, Iwashi is responsible for collecting and analyzing data on the status of all the participants, and making reports to his superiors as necessary. His only concern is collecting accurate data, so he does not interpose his own personal judgments.

Tayuya: A member of the Oto no Yoninshu (Sound 4). Age: 14. Female. The only Female. member of the group. However, the curse words she hurls around and her arrogant attitude are not very lady-like. She can perform Kuchiyose and Genjustu with her sole weapon, a flute. She knows a number of types of Genjutsu.

Tazuna: A resident of the Land of Waves. Age: 59. Male. Tazuna is a bridge-builder who wants to construct a bridge connecting the Land of Waves with the continent and restore the connection that Gato had severed; Tazuna completes the job, despite the threat to his own life.

Teguse: A resident of the Land of Waves. A pick-pocket. Age: 44. Male. Thief who operates in the Land of Waves. Tries to rob Sakura, but she mistakes him for a simple pervert and brings him down with a mighty kick.

Temari: A Ninja from Sunagakure. Genin. Age: 15. Female. Temari is the daughter of the Kazekage, who is the leader of Sunagakure, and the older sister of Gaara and Kankuro. Her strong-willed disposition and stormy temper are entirely befitting for a sibling of Gaara. The huge folding fan she carries at all times can be used for attack or defense, and she specializes in wind techniques.

Tenten: A Ninja from Konohagakure. Genin. Age: 13. Female. A female Ninja teamed with Rock Lee and Neji Hyuga. Like her teammates, she is better at Taijutsu than Ninjutsu. She is particularly good at attacks using Ninja weapons, and keeps a variety of gear hidden on her body. During the Chunin exam, she loses to Temari.

Teuchi: A resident of Konohagakure. Age: 43. Male. The owner of Ichiraku, the ramen shop Naruto frequents. A 30-year veteran chef, he creates delicious ramen through thorough attention to details, proficiency, and his love for the dish

Tobio: A Ninja from Konohagakure. Genin. Age: 12. Male. At the Ninja Academy graduation briefing, he inadvertently pushes Naruto from behind, resulting in his kiss with Sasuke.

Tobitake Tonbo: A Ninja from Konohagakure. Age: 27. Male. It's hard to read Tonbo's expressions since the top part of his face is bandaged up. He seems to take great pride in his position and work, and if this pride is wounded, he takes great offense.

Tonton: Pet piglet kept by Tsunade. The pig and Tsunade always wear matching outfits. The pig is not only cute, it is also as brave as its master, and helps Tsunade during the battle with Orochimaru.

Toriichi Kumade: A Ninja from Konohagakure. Tokubetsu Jonin. Age: 29. Male. While working as a spy in Kirigakure, he encounters former Anbu member Zabuza. He is killed almost immediately by Zabuza's Silent Killing Technique.

Tsubaki: A resident of Konohagakure. A home-maker. When Naruto is depressed, having failed his final exams, far from taking pity on him, she showers him with abuse. Friends with Ibara.

Tsuchino: A student at the Sunagakure Ninja Academy. Age: 12. Male. When he was six, he had his legs broken by Gaara's sand.

Tsunade: A Ninja from Konohagakure. The fifth Hokage. Age: 50. Female. Tsunade and Jiraiya, along with Orochimaru, are known as the Legendary Three Ninja. She is the grandchild of the first Hokage. After the showdown with Orochimaru in which the third Hokage dies, she becomes the fifth Hokage on the recommendation of Jiraiya. She has exceptional Ninjutsu and Taijutsu skills, but is particularly good at medical techniques.

Tsunami: A resident of the Land of Waves. Age: 29. Inari's mother. When Inari is attacked by Gato's men, she risks her life to protect him. She also cares for Kakashi after he passes out from overusing his Chakra.

Tsurugi Misumi: A Ninja from Otogakure. Age: 23. Male. Participates in the Chunin exams as a spy on Orochimaru's orders. Defeated by Kankuro during the exam. He can perform unusual techniques that use his entire body as a weapon, and has been altered so that he can effortlessly contort any part of his body.

U

Uchiha Fugaku: A Ninja from Konohagakure. Jonin. Male. Itachi and Sasuke's father. The head of the Keimu Butai (Konoha Military Police Force). As the head of the Uchiha Clan, he wears his family insignia with pride and strives to ensure the prosperity of the clan.

Uchiha Inabi: A Ninja from Konohagakure. Age: 25. Male. An elite operative in the Keimu Butai (Konoha Military Police Force). Often cautioned the young Itachi about his suspicious behavior which led to friction between the two.

Uchiha Itachi: A member of the high-ranking Uchiha Clan from Konohagkure. Male. Sasuke's brother. A disturbed genius, he carried out the annihilation of his clan with his own hands. The tragic story of Itachi and his clan is well known in the village, but his current whereabouts and state of mind are a mystery. Possesses a prodigal eye called the Mangekyo Sharingan (lit. Kaleidoscopic Copy Wheel Eye) which is rare even among the Uchiha Clan..

Uchiha Mikoto: A Ninja from Konohagakure. Jonin. Female. Itachi and Sasuke's mother. While the head of the family, Fugaku, is a rather strict father figure always thinking of the Uchiha Clan name, Mikoto is the epitome of a warm, caring mother. She loves Itachi and Sasuke equally, not because they are Uchiha Clan members, but because they are her sons.

Uchiha Obito: A Ninja from Konohagakure. Male. Hatake Kakashi's contemporary. Although proud of his status as a member of the Uchiha Clan, he is troubled by his lack of abilities. Highly values his friends and laid down his life for one. This has a huge influence on Kakashi's outlook on life.

Uchiha Sasuke: A Ninja from Konohagakure. Genin. Age: 13. Male. In keeping with his status as member of the Uchiha Clan he graduates from the Ninja Academy at the top of his class and is closely watched from all sides with expectation or jealousy. The brother he formerly looked up to, Itachi, murdered his family, and he now lives for the sole purpose of exacting revenge on him. He is friends and classmates with Naruto, but fears his growing strength, and resents him for it. Possesses the Sharingan (Copy Wheel Eye) and is skilled at Katon (Fire Release) techniques. Learns the secret technique of Chidori (Thousand Birds) from Kakashi. Has a Juin (Cursed Seal) implanted in him by Orochimaru and, mesmerized by its power, leaves the village to find its author.

Uchiha Shisui: A Ninja from Konohagakure. Male. A member of the Uchiha Clan whom Itachi loved like an older brother. He notices Itachi's change and keeps an eye on him, but then dies in a mysterious suicide. It seems highly likely that Itachi was somehow involved in this suicide.

Uchiha Tekka: A Ninja from Konohagakure. Age: 21. Male. Works for the Keimu Butai (Konoha Military Police Force). Within the unit he cuts a modest figure but his passion and pride towards the Uchiha Clan are no less than the others.

Uchiha Teyaki: A resident of Konohagakure. Age: 46. Male. Owner of the Senbei (rice cracker) shop, Uchiha Senbei. He takes great pride in his well-established business which he has been managing since it first opened. He remains faithful to the secret recipe of the crackers handed down through the generations.

Uchiha Uruchi: A resident of Konohagakure. Age: 46. A female employee of the Senbei (rice cracker) shop, Uchiha Senbei. Each Senbei is baked with loving care and their rich taste is popular with the kids.

Uchiha Yashiro: A Ninja from Konohagakure. Age: 45. Male. A senior law-enforcing agent for the Keimu Butai (Konoha Military Police Force). With astute analytical powers, he is strong leader to the other members of the unit and is greatly respected even by Uchiha Fukagu, the head of the clan.

Udon: A student at the Konohagakure Ninja Academy. Age: 8. Male. A friend of Konohamaru who looks up to Naruto as a leader.

Ugai: A Ninja from Konohagakure. Age: 22. Male. Member of a medical team. When Lee is taken into hospital he takes Guy to Tsunade. As a medical Ninja he is still a novice. However, he is methodical and earnest, so is an excellent doctor in the making.

Umino Iruka: A Ninja from Konohagakure. Chunin. Age: 23. A well-loved teacher at the Ninja Academy with a genuine passion for his work. He is also very popular with Naruto. His love of teaching stems from the lonely childhood spent after both his parents were killed by the Nine-Tailed Fox Spirit. Witnessed the fourth Lord Hokage laying down his life for the safety of the village which had a shaping effect on his character. He always thinks of those around him.

Utatane Koharu: A member of the Konoha Goikenban (Advisory Council). The Goikenban's mission is to guide and support Lord Hokage in his role as the leader of the village. Like Homaru, another Goikennban member, he has been in position for a long time. Offers advice in all matters to help Lord Hokage make balanced judgments.

Utsuki Yugao: A Ninja from Konohagakure. Member of the Anbu. Female. Pretty, well-featured Kunoichi (female Ninja). When she swears revenge for the death of her lover Gekkou Yahate, she takes off her mask (the symbol of the Anbu) and exposes her true face..

Uzumaki Naruto: A Ninja from Konohagakure. Genin. Age: 13. Male. Main character of the story. Just after he was born the Nine-Tailed Fox Spirit was imprisoned in his body. Since then he has carried the weight of his destiny on his back and continued his solitary battle. Cherishes the dream of one day becoming the strongest Lord Hokage, and always believes in his own abilities. A courageous young Ninja who never retreats, however bad the situation is. His courage exerts a powerful influence on the people he meets. While not especially gifted at Ninja techniques, he is occasionally able to draw on the Chakra of the fox spirit within him. At these times he can attack with an overwhelming power. Currently training intensively to master the advanced Rasengan (Spiraling Sphere) technique that the fourth Lord Hokage pioneered.

Y

Yakushi Kabuto: A Ninja from the village of Otogakure. Age: 20. Male. Pretends to be a Ninja from Konohagakure, but is actually working as a spy for Orochimaru, gathering data on the other Ninja in the village. Has extremely advanced healing techniques, which surprise even Tsunade.

Yamanaka Ino: A Ninja from Konohagakure. Genin. Age: 13. Female. Works in a team known as the Inoshikacho Trio with Shikamaru and Choji. She has a selfish and competitive nature. However, she was kind to Sakura when she was being bullied at the academy so has a kind side to her character. Now she is both Sakura's friend and rival for Sasuke's attention.

Yamanaka Inoichi: A Ninja from Konohagakure. Jonin. Age: 38. Male. Ino's

father. Skilled at Genjutsu in which he steals inside his opponent's mind and manipulates their will. Along with Choza and Shikaku he made up part of the three man cell known as the Inoshikacho Trio.

Yashamaru: A Ninja from Sunagakure. Chunin. Age: 27. Female. Gaara's aunt on his mother's side. A medical Ninja who looked after Gaara from an early age under orders from Lord Kazekage. However, she still holds some resentment against Gaara whose birth was the cause of her sister's death. As Gaara grows Lord Kazekage begins to fear him and decides to have him assassinated. He orders Yashamaru to carry out his plan. She obeys and tries to kill Gaara, but loses her own life instead.

Yuhi Kurenai: A Ninja from Konohagakure. Jonin. Age: 28. Female. Generally a head-strong Kunoichi (female Ninja), she also has an innocent side to her and she blushed when Kakashi was teasing her about her and Sarutobi Asuma. She is skilled at Genjutsu, and although she lost, she displayed an equal level of Genjutsu skill during her fight with Itachi.

Z

Zaku Abumi: A Ninja from Otogakure. Age: 14. Male. He joins the Oto Ninja, and takes the Chunin exam at Orochimaru's behest. He has an aggressive personality, and not infrequently overestimates his own abilities. Zaku's pride stems from the fact that he considers himself a member of the elite, having been chosen by Orochimaru. He lives to serve Orochimaru, and never doubts that he will achieve recognition.

Zori: Samurai who works as Gato's bodyguard. A cold-blooded killer, as long as he gets paid he'll kill anyone, including children; his particular "skills" indicate the kind of slaughter he's been involved in. He tries to kidnap Tsunami on Gato's orders, but is defeated by Naruto's Ninjutsu.

GLOSSARY(JUTSU)

A

Amagumo (lit. Rain of Spiders): One of Kidomaru's techniques. He summons a giant spider, which produces countless baby spiders that ensnare the target in their webbing. The web spun by the babies is made of Chakra, and hard to escape from once the victim is caught.

Amaterasu (lit. Heavenly Light): A technique used by Itachi Uchiha. It produces pitch black flames which burn continuously for seven days. The details of this technique are largely unknown.

B

Baika no Jutsu (lit. Doubling Technique): A secret Ninjutsu technique of the Akimichi clan. Allows the user to expand their body at will, and withdraw their arms, legs and head like a turtle.

Bubun Baika no Jutsu (lit. Partial Doubling Technique): Technique that creates illusory clones in the user's image. Because the clones are illusions, they cannot perform attacks. This technique is used solely to confuse the enemy. It is a basic Ninja technique.

Bunshin no Jutsu (lit. Clone Technique): Technique that creates illusory clones in the user's image. Because the clones are illusions, they cannot perform attacks. This technique is used solely to con-

fuse the enemy. It is a basic Ninja technique.

Bunshin Taiatari (lit. Clone Body Blow): Apprentice Gardner. Age: 13. Male. When he sees Shimeji at work in the villages near Tanzaku Town, he is so impressed that he decides to become his apprentice. His ambition is to become a world-class gardener and works hard everyday to realize that goal.

Byakugan (lit. White Eye): The Hyuga Clan's Kekkeigenkai. Those who posses the Byakugan have incredible vision and can see through flesh.

C

Chidori (lit. Thousand Birds): The user concentrates a huge amount of Chakra in one arm, then gets a long, running start at their target, allowing them to deliver a fast, lunging attack of unparalleled power. A technique invented by Kakashi, who teaches it to Sasuke.

Chikatsu Saisei no Jutsu (Healing Resuscitation Regeneration Technique): A medical technique. A part of the patient's body is used to heal the injured part by shifting the ratio of healthy cells. Controlling one's Chakra in order to fine tune the cell ratios is very difficult, so this technique requires a lot of time.

Chodan Bakugeki (lit. Bullet Butterfly Bomb): Chakra is concentrated in the left user's hand and takes on a unique, beautiful shape before being plunged into the opponent. It has incredible destructive power, but is dangerous to the user as well as the victim.

D

Daikamaitachi no Jutsu (lit. Great Cutting Whirlwind Technique): One of Temari's techniques. She creates a strong, turbulent wind, then summons Kamaitachi which rides the gust, slicing up anything in its path. She simultaneously uses a sound spell to nullify any Genjutsu the opponent might be using.

Daisan no Me (lit. Third Eye): A technique used exclusively by Gaara. An eye made out of sand is created, and connected to Gaara by an optic nerve created from Chakra, so that Gaara can see whatever the sand eye sees. He can send the eye to distant places in order to conduct surveillance.

Dokugiri (lit. Poison Mist): The user's Chakra is transformed into poison, which is sprayed from the mouth in a fine mist.

Doton: Dochu Eigyo no Jutsu (lit. Earth Release: Underground Projection Fish Technique): Ninjutsu that allows the user to hide underground, then pop up to perform a surprise attack.

Doton: Doroku Gaeshi (lit. Earth Release: Earth Shore Return): One of Jirobo's techniques. He lifts up a section of earth, creating a wall in front of him, blocking enemy attacks.

Doton: Doryu Dango (lit. Earth Release: Earth Mausoleum Dumpling): Using a combination of Chakra and sheer strength, Jirobo can pick up a huge piece of earth and slam it down on his victims.

Doton: Doryu Heki (lit. Earth Release: Earth Flow Rampart): Creates a hard shield of earth, protecting the user from attacks. Because the earth is made of Chakra emitted by the user, this technique can be used inside buildings and other places where there is no earth around.

Doton: Iwayado Kuzushi (lit. Earth Release: Rock Lodging Cave-in): The victim is led into a cave, which is then caused to collapse, burying them alive. A specialty of the Iwagakure Ninja.

Doton Kekkai: Dorodomu (lit. Earth Release Barrier: Dungeon Chamber of Nothingness): Creates a huge dome of earth inside of which opponents are trapped. The user can siphon off the Chakra of trapped prisoners.

Doton: Retsudotensho (lit. Earth Release: Split Earth Turn Around Palm): A basic technique of the Iwagakure Ninja. Chakra is concentrated in the palm of the hand and used to open up fissures in the earth.

Doton: Shinjuzanshu no Jutsu (lit. Earth Release: Inner Decapitation Technique): The hidden user pulls the target into the earth. The user then attacks the immobilized enemy.

F

Fuja Hoin (Evil Sealing Method): Technique used by Kakashi to close the curse seal applied to Sasuke by Orochimaru.

Fuka Hoin (lit. Fire Sealing Method):
One method of sealing used for specialized purposes. This one is optimized for Katon techniques. If an opponent attempts to use a Katon technique, the technique itself will be blocked by the seal.

Fukoku Hoin (lit. Black Sealing Method)
Technique used to shift Sasuke's cursed seal to level 2.

Fushitensei (lit. Living Corpse Reincarnation): Allows the user to transfer their consciousness into other bodies, effectively making them immortal. Perfected by Orochimaru over many years of experimentation.

Futon: Daitoppa (lit. Wind Release: Great Breakthrough): The user creates wind with his Chakra, and slams it into the enemy.

Futon: Mugen Sajin Daitoppa (lit. Wind Release: Infinite Sand Cloud Great Breakthrough): Gaara uses this when transformed into Shukaku. He sucks in air through his mouth, and spews it out with Chakra-imbued sand. This attack is easily strong enough to chop down huge trees with.

Futon: Renkudan (lit. Wind Release: Drilling Air Bullet): Gaara uses this when transformed into Shukaku. He beats his belly and spits out a very high pressure ball of air from his mouth. The ball of air contains a large amount of Chakra, and explodes on impact.

G

Garoga (lit. Double Wolf Fang) :
One of Inuzuka Kiba's techniques. He first uses Jinju Konbi Henge: Sotoro (Man-Beast Fusion Transformation: Double-Headed Wolf) with Akamaru to form the two-headed wolf. He then performs a high-speed spinning attack.

Gatsuga (lit. Double Piercing Fang):
One of Inuzuka Kiba's signature techniques. An esoteric use of the Jujintaijutsu, in which Kiba in his bestial form, and Akamaru in his Kiba form, shower their target with multiple, spinning attacks. The force of the attack can reduce boulders to rubble.

Gogyo Fuin (lit. Five Elements Seal):
A seal Orochimaru uses to nullify the effect of the Shisho Fuin (Four Symbols Seal) that the fourth Lord Hokage placed on Naruto to seal away the fox spirit while allowing Naruto to freely use its Chakra. By placing the odd-numbered Five Elements Seal on top of the even-numbered Four Symbols Seal, Orochimaru effectively eliminated Naruto's ability to obtain the Fox Spirit's Chakra.

Gogyo Kain (lit. Five Elements Unseal): An unsealing technique Jiraiya uses to undo Orochimaru's Gogyo Fuin, which had been preventing Naruto from using the Fox Spirit's Chakra. It is an advanced technique and can only be used by Ninja of Jiariya's class.

Gokusamaiso (lit. Prison Sand Burial)
A technique used by Gaara. Instantly pulverizes the ground under the target's feet into sand. The hapless victim is sucked into the

sand.

H

Hakke no Fuinshiki (lit. Eight Trigrams Sealing Ritual): When the fourth Lord Hokage sealed the Fox Spirit inside of Naruto, he uses two Shisho Fuin (Four Symbols Seals) to do the job. He left a small crack between the two seals so that the Fox Spirit's Chakra would be available to Naruto. This arrangement of seals is called the Hakke no Fuinshiki.

Hakke Rokujuyon Sho (lit. Eight Trigrams Sixty-Four Palms): A technique of the main house of the Hyuga Clan. Neji, a branch family member, figures it out using intuition and talent alone. This attack paralyzes the victim by striking 64 of the Chakra holes located on the body.

Haimaru San Kyodai (Three Haimaru Brothers): The three Ninja Dogs which work with Inuzuka Hana (Kiba's older sister). Normally gentle and quiet, when they get into battle they attack the enemy with great fighting spirit.

Hakkesho Kaiten (lit. Eight Trigram Palms Heavenly Spin): aijutsu in which the user unleashes a large amount of Chakra from one of their Chakra holes, stopping enemy attacks and allowing the user to perform flips and jumps. The technique is a secret of the main house of the Hyuga Clan, but Neji mastered it independently, despite being from a branch family.

Haremu no Jutsu (lit. Harem Technique): An original technique created by Naruto. Combines his Oiroke no Jutsu (Ninja Centerfold – Viz), which allows him to become a beautiful naked woman, with the Taju Kage Bunshin no Jutsu (lit. Multiple Shadow Clone Technique). It incapacitates most adult males by surrounding them with beautiful naked women.

Hari Jizo (Needle Jizo): A technique used by Jiraiya. His own hairs stiffen into needles, repelling enemy attacks.

Henge: Kongonyoi (Transformation: Adamantine Staff): A transformation technique used by Enma, the third Lord Hokage's comrade. He transforms his body into a staff, which becomes a weapon for the third Lord Hokage. Because it is a living weapon, it can attack autonomously.

Henge no Jutsu (Transformation Technique): Technique that allows the user to transform into another person and get nearer to the enemy. It is very useful for gathering information during battles, and is a fundamental Ninjutsu technique.

Hien (lit. Flying Swallow): Technique that boosts the killing power of bladed weapons, such as Kunai and swords, with Chakra.

Hiraishin no Jutsu (lit. Flying Thunder God Technique): This technique is the specialty of the fourth Lord Hokage, and earned him the name Konoha no Kiiroi Senko (lit. Konoha's Yellow Flash).

I

Infuin: Kai (lit. Shadow Seal: Release): A technique Tsunade uses in order to perform her extremely powerful Sozosaisei, healing technique. Infuin: Kai is available when Tsunade has a large amount of Chakra stored in her body. The Sozosaisei technique itself also requires a huge amount of Chakra, so Tsunade has placed a seal on her own forehead to store the necessary Chakra.

In'yu Shometsu (lit. Shadow Wound Removal): Allows a user to cast a healing technique on part of his or her body before being attacked. Used by Kabuto, a character with much experience in medical techniques.

J

Joro Senbon (lit. Sprinkling Needles): A technique that uses Senbon (a needle-like Ninja weapon). Countless Senbon are launched high into the air from a special umbrella, which is twirled to launch them over a wide area. When the Senbon fall back to earth, the user can use Chakra to control them so they rain down on the target's head. A technique used by Shigure, a Ninja from Amegakure.

Juinjustu (lit. Cursed Seal Techniques): Refers to the cursed seals Orochimaru applies to those he considers talented. The application process is extremely painful, and only a few survive it. While the seals allow the user to tap their Chakra without limits, giving them terrifying power, it makes them Orochimaru's slave. The main house of the Hyuga Clan also apply cursed seals to members of branch families.

Jujin Bunshin (lit. Half-Beast Clone): This is a technique used by Inuzuka Kiba, and is the basis for many techniques performed in conjunction with his Ninken, Akamaru. Gijin Ninpo is used to transform Akamaru into a copy of Kiba, while Kiba takes on a bestial form; both master and dog look like Kiba in his bestial form. Unlike the Kage Bunshin technique, it does not require a huge amount of Chakra, but can be used to obtain similar effects.

K

Kage Bunshin no Jutsu (lit. Shadow Clone Technique) : The clones created by normal Bunshin techniques are mere illusions, but the Kage Bunshin clones are real, and each capable of performing physical attacks. This technique is used by Naruto frequently.

Kage Buyo (lit. Shadow of the Dancing Leaf): A technique used to slip behind and follow a target, like a shadow. Although this seems like it should be easy, it's actually rather difficult to pull off without being noticed, and is particularly hard for Genin.

Kage Kubi Shibari no Jutsu (lit. Shadow Strangle Technique): A secret technique of the Nara clan, it is similar to Kagemane no Jutsu, but more practical for use in battle. The user directly damages the enemy by manipulating a shadow imbued with physical power.

Kagemane no Jutsu (lit. Shadow Imitation Technique): The user can lengthen their shadow until it connects with that of an opponent, after which the user's motions control the opponent. The technique itself does no damage, but as it can immobilize even the strongest enemy, it is a particularly effective attack in team situations. Shikamaru is the character most adept at this technique.

Kage Shuriken no Jutsu (lit. Shadow Shuriken Technique): Two Shuriken are stacked and thrown together, so that one obscures the other, giving the impression of just one Shuriken. Even if the first Shuriken is successfully blocked, the second one hits its target.

Kakuremino no Jutsu (lit. Cloak of Invisibility Technique): A technique Konohamaru uses when shadowing Naruto. The user carries a piece of cloth patterned to look like a wall etc. When in danger of being discovered, the user conceals him or herself behind the fabric and blends in with the background scenery.

Kamaitachi no Jutsu (lit. Cutting Whirlwind Technique): One of Temari's techniques. Temari uses her giant fan to produce gusts of wind, which interact with normal air currents to form a vortex; anyone caught in this wind is sliced up by countless invisible blades. It can also be used as a defense against missile weapons.

Kanashibari no Jutsu (lit. Temporary Paralysis Technique): A binding technique in which the user creates thread-like strands of Chakra that ensnare and immobilize the victim. This is a basic technique that even Genin can use, but at the Jonin level it can be used to bind multiple targets.

Karamatsu no Mai (lit. Dance of the Larch): Technique used by Kimimaro that allows him to grow bones from anywhere on his body. The bones, which are needle-sharp, will cut through the flesh of anyone who touches them.

Kasumi Jusha no Jutsu (lit. Mist Servant Technique): Creepy, dark Ninja appear from the midst of trees and rocks close in on the target. They are slow, but multiply when hit, making them a useful psychological weapon.

Katon: Gamayu Endan (lit. Fire Release: Toad Oil Flame Bullet): A cooperative attack using oil stored in Gamabunta's body and a Katon technique. The user creates flames and directs at the target while Gamabunta spews oil at it. The firepower of the average Katon technique is increased by adding oil.

Katon: Gokakyu no Jutsu (lit. Fire Release: Great Fireball Technique): The user's Chakra is shaped and converted into fire within the user's body and is spat out in the shape of a giant sphere. The extent of the effect depends on the amount of Chakra used. One of Sasuke's techniques

Katon: Hosenka no Jutsu (lit. Fire Release: Phoenix Immortal Fire Technique): Like the seedpods of the hosenka (jewelweed) plant, which, when touched, burst, spewing out seeds, the user spits fireballs in every direction.

Katon: Ryuka no Jutsu (lit. Fire Release: Dragon Fire Technique): The user breaths a torrent of flame that travels in a straight line and burns the target.

Kawarimi no Jutsu (lit. Body Replacement Technique): When attacked, the user can instantaneously switch places with another object; the object is hit instead, briefly giving the impression that the attack was successful. It is one of the basic techniques used by Ninja in Naruto.

Kaze no Yaiba (lit. Blade of Wind): The user creates a blade of Chakra with his fingertips and hurls it at the opponent.

Kekkai Hojin (lit. Barrier Encampment Method): Sheets of paper with written incantations are placed on trees, rocks etc. to form a perimeter. The instant someone steps within that perimeter, a trap is activated.

Kikaichu no Jutsu (lit. Destruction Bug Host Technique): An esoteric technique of the Aburame clan, who act as hosts for the parasitic bugs; in exchange for providing the bugs with a steady supply of Chakra, the hosts gain control over them. The countless bugs can be used to attack enemies or gather information.

Kirigakure no Jutsu (lit. Mist Hiding Technique): A technique used by Ninja from the village of Kirigakure. Chakra is combined with water to create a mist that can be used to hide the user, and allows them to suddenly appear, as if out of nowhere.

Kisei Kikai no Jutsu (lit. Parasite Demon Destruction Technique): A technique that can only be used by Sakon's older twin, Ukon. He uses Chakra to enter a target body by combining with it at a cellular level. He can then destroy the host's cells to the point where they die.

Kokuangyo no Jutsu (Bringer-of-darkness Technique): Genjutsu that causes the illusion of complete darkness around the target. The victims will see only darkness, and be totally blinded.

Kongo Roheki (lit. Adamantine Prison Wall): A Ninja from Konohagakure. Enma transforms into a staff (Kongonyoi), clones himself, and fences in his opponent.

Konoha Daisenpu (lit. Leaf Great Whirlwind): A combo consisting of a low-kick, middle-kick, high-kick and finally an axe-kick performed in one, fluid motion. Lee is adept at this technique.

Konoha Gorikki Senpu (lit. Leaf Strong Whirlwind): A technique used by Might Guy, who is the number one Taijutsu practitioner in Konoha. It consists of a reverse spinning kick that embodies all the secrets of Taijutsu. Because he spins faster than the eye can see, it is impossible to dodge.

Konoha Reppu (lit. Leaf Gale): This is a basic Taijutsu technique, but in Lee's hands it's as destructive as a high-level technique. It consists of a simple reverse sweep-kick, but Lee's speed and power give it enough force to send big opponents flying.

Konoha Senpu (lit. Konoha Hurricane): A high and low kick delivered in succession while spinning. Lee is adept at this technique. The alternating of high and low attacks causes the target to rock back and forth.

Kori Shinchu no Jutsu (lit. Sly Mind Affect Technique): Genjutsu that induces the victim to retrace the same path over and over, as if lost in a labyrinth. It can be cast on multiple people at the same time. The victims do not notice they're bewitched, and will continue walking in circles indefinitely.

Kyomeisen (lit. Vibrating Sound Drill): A technique used by Dosu Kinuta. He uses the sound attack from the device on his right arm to damage the victim's inner ear, causing them to lose their sense of balance.

Kuchiyose: Doton: Tsuiga no Jutsu (lit. Summoning: Earth Release: Tracking Fang Technique): Summons a number of Ninja Dogs, who appear from under the ground and chase the enemy. This is a high level tracking and attack technique, and if timed correctly, the dogs will pounce simultaneously.

Kugutsu no Jutsu (Puppet Technique): The user produces threads of Chakra from the fingertips and uses them to control inanimate puppets, making them appear to be alive. This technique demands a high level of skill, as the user is constantly using Chakra over long periods. Kankuro is the character most adept at this technique.

Kuchiyose: Edo Tensei (lit. Summoning: Impure World Resurrection): A Kuchiyose technique only Orochimaru can use. A forbidden technique that resurrects a deceased person. A living human is sacrificed to summon the spirit of the dead person. This technique has been kept secret due to its horrific nature.

Kuchiyose: Gamaguchi Shibari (lit. Summoning: Toad Mouth Bind): A bizarre technique that summons just the esophagus from a giant toad that lives in the heart of Mount Myomokuzan. Enemies are trapped inside the esophagus. Only Jiraiya can use this technique.

Kuchiyose: Kirikirimai (lit. Cutting Dance): A powerful technique, in which Temari controls the wind with her giant fan. She creates a strong wind, then summons Kamaitachi which ride the gust, slicing up anything in their path. The radius of effect is several hundred meters, and the technique is powerful enough to destroy a whole forest.

Kuchiyose no Jutsu (lit. Summoning Technique): A type of time-space manipulation Ninjutsu in which the user signs a contract in his or her own blood to gain the ability to summon an animal whenever needed. The summoned animal will help the user in any situation - whether it involves fighting or fleeing.

Kuchiyose: Rashomon (lit. Summoning: Rashomon): Summons a sturdy gate, which protects the user from physical attacks.

Kumo Mayu (Spider Cocoon): One of Kidomaru's techniques. He traps enemies inside a cocoon of spider webbing, and crushes them to death.

Kumo Nenkin (lit. Spider Sticky Gold): One of Kidomaru's techniques. He spits out spider webbing that hardens like metal and forms it into arrows which fires at enemies.

Kumo Nento (lit. Spider Sticking Spit): One of Kidomaru's techniques. He makes a rope with the threads he spits out of his mouth, uses it to snare enemies, and swings them around with it.

Kumo Shibari (lit. Spider Bind): One of Kidomaru's techniques. He throws a mesh composed of Chakra strands at attacking enemies, netting them like fish.

Kumo Soka (lit. Spider Web Flower): One of Kidomaru's techniques. He produces a sticky thread from his mouth and uses it to snare enemies.

Kumo Sokai (lit. Spider Web Unfold): One of Kidomaru's techniques, in which he produces a spider web in front of him to trap oncoming enemies.

Kumosenkyu Suzaku (lit. Spider War Bow Tremendous Fissure): One of Kidomaru's techniques. He fires on enemies with a special bow. The arrows remain connected to his mouth by a strand of Chakra, allowing him to control them, resulting in a 120% hit-rate.

Kurohigi Kiki Ippatsu (lit. Black Secret Technique Machine One Shot): A puppet technique used by Kankuro which uses his two puppets – Karasu for attack and Kuroari for entrapment – at the same time. Kuroari traps the victim, who is then skewered by Karasu's seven blades.

M

Magen: Jubaku Satsu (lit. Demonic Illusion: Tree Bind Death): An ancient Genjutsu of Konohagakure, it paralyzes victims by convincing them they are being held by a living tree.

Magen: Kokoni Arazu no Jutsu (lit. Demonic Illusion: False Surroundings Technique): Makes the victim think they are somewhere other than where they actually are. Can be cast on a wide area, so that anyone who enters that area will become disoriented.

Magen: Kyoten Chiten (lit. Demonic Illusion: Mirror of Heaven and Earth Change): Reflects any Genjutsu, causing it to be applied to the person who cast it. This is one way to counter Genjutsu, but it requires the ability to discern that a Genjutsu is being cast. As a result, only possessors of the Sharingan can use it.

Magen: Narakumi no Jutsu (lit. Demonic Illusion: Hell Viewing Technique): Everyone has some fear or phobia. This technique reads that fear, and causes it to appear realistically before the victim. Kakashi is adept at this technique.

Makyo Hyo Sho (Demonic Ice Mirrors -Viz): This technique creates mirrors of ice around the opponent. The reflected images are not merely confusing to the enemy; the user can attack the reflections themselves. This is a technique of Haku's clan and is enshrouded in mystery.

Mangekyo Sharingan (lit. Kaleidoscope Copy Wheel Eye): A specialized form of the Uchiha clan's Sharingan. The possessor's insightfulness and hypnotic abilities are an order of magnitude higher, and they can use techniques, such as Tsukuyomi, which cannot be used with the normal Sharingan.

Mateki: Genbuso Kyoku (lit. Magic Flute: Control Song of the Phantom Warriors): Ninjutsu technique with which Tayuya controls the three Doki demons she summons.

Mateki: Mugenonsa (lit. Magic Flute: Dream Sound Chain): A Genjutsu that relies on the sound from a flute. Those that hear the flute's melody feel as if they are bound with strong cords, and cannot move. Also makes the victims hallucinate; they see their very arms melting away, making this an effective psychological weapon.

Meisai Gakure no Jutsu (lit. Camouflaged Hiding Technique): The user can control the light reflected from their body, making them seem to appear and disappear.

Mikazuki no Mai (lit. Dance of the Crescent Moon): Creates three clones, who attack the opponent simultaneously. It is extremely fast and impossible to dodge. While it may be possible to avoid one of the attacks, getting hit just once results in a mortal wound.

Mizu Bunshin no Jutsu (lit. Water Clone Technique): Creates a copy of the user composed of water. Like the Shadow Clones, they have a physical presence and can perform attacks. Zabuza is adept at this technique.

Mokuton Hijutsu: Jukai Korin (lit. Wood Release Secret Technique: Birth of Dense Woodland): An advanced technique of the first Lord Hokage. Allows the user to create and control a large tree using their Chakra.

Mushi Bunshin no Jutsu (lit. Bug Clone Technique): The user collects many thousands or tens of thousands of insects in one place, and forms them into a copy of the user. This is an esoteric technique is used by Shino Aburame.

N

Nan no Kaizo (Soft Physique Modification): Makes the user's body flexible and elastic, allowing them to stretch their torso or neck unnatural distances.

Nawanuke no Jutsu (lit. Rope Escape Technique): A technique used when the user has been tied up with a rope. The user dislocates a joint to escape. One of the first techniques taught at the Ninja Academy of Konohagakure. A fundamental Ninjutsu technique.

Nehan Shoja no Jutsu (lit. Temple of Nirvana Technique): Genjutsu that creates the illusion of dancing, white feathers. Anyone who sees these fluttering feathers becomes entranced and falls into a deep sleep.

Nenkin no Yoroi (lit. Armor of Sticky Gold): One of Kidomaru's techniques. He oozes Kumo Nenkin, which becomes metal on contact with air, from his sweat glands, covering his body in a metallic coating.

Nikudan Hari Sensha (Spiked Human Bullet Tank): Akimichi Choji performs his Nikudan Sensha technique, but uses weapons to increase its effectiveness. Choji wraps himself in Kunai attached to strings, which serve as spikes when he performs the Nikudan Sensha. The Kunai inflict grievous damage when he strikes his target.

Nikudan Sensha (lit. Meat Tank): One of Choji's techniques. Taking advantage of his hefty body, he rolls into opponents at high speed. The perfect technique for Choji, as it allows him to turn his weight into offensive power.

O

Oboro Bunshin no Jutsu (lit. Haze Clone Technique): A technique used by Ninja from Amegakure Village. At first glance this appears to be a standard clone technique, but in fact the clones are used as a distraction.

Oiroke no Jutsu (Ninja Centerfold – Viz): An original technique created by Naruto. Naruto contrives this technique as a way to distract other guys; he transforms himself into a beautiful, naked woman. Any men who see him in this form are butter in his hands.

Omote Renge (lit. Front Lotus): One of Lee's Taijutsu techniques. Lee sends his opponent flying with a kick, wraps his arm bandages around his enemy in mid-air, grabs onto them, then slams them head-first into the earth while spinning.

R

Raikiri (Lightning Cut): Among Kakashi's thousand or so copied techniques, this is one he thought of himself. He creates a ball of Chakra so powerful it can be seen with the naked eye, then plunges it into his enemy's chest. It turns Kakashi's arm into an unparalleled sword. It is a very simple but very destructive technique. This fits with Kakashi's "simple is better" philosophy.

Rakanken (lit. Achiever of Nirvana Fist): One of Jirobo's techniques. It uses his immense size to his advantage.

Ranshinsho (lit. Bodily Confusion Attack): The user converts their Chakra into electricity and uses it to disrupt the nervous system of their opponent, who loses control of his or her body. Medical Ninja are adept at this technique, as they have a good knowledge of the human body.

Rasengan (lit. Spiraling Sphere): The user focuses Chakra energy into the palm of the hand, compresses it by spinning it violently, then shoots it at their enemy. This technique took the fourth Lord Hokage three years to perfect. It works on simple principles and can be fired quickly. Its power depends on the level of the user; for high-level Ninja it has the destructive force of a hurricane.

Ryusa Bakuryu (lit. Desert Quicksand Torrent): Gaara's knockout technique. Gaara uses the sand he carries to erode the surface of the ground, creating a patch of desert which then turns into a huge wave of sand.

S

Sabaku Fuyu (lit. Desert Suspension): A technique that creates a floating mass of sand that can be ridden. One of Gaara's techniques.

Sabaku Kyu, (lit. Desert Coffin): One of Gaara's favored techniques. Gaara uses the sand in the gourd he wears on his back to bury and trap opponents. Because the attack uses sand, Gaara can freely change its form, and use it in defensive moves too. Whether the trapped victim lives or dies is up to Gaara.

Sabaku Soso (lit. Desert Funeral): A horrifying technique that Gaara uses to crush victims caught by his Sabaku Kyu attack. The pressure exerted by the sand equals several tons from all directions, crushing opponents in an instant.

Sabaku Taiso (lit. Desert Imperial Funeral): Uses the terrifying Sabaku Soso which crushes opponents, but applies it to a wider area.

Sawarabi no Mai (lit. Dance of the Seedling Fern): Kimimaro's final technique. Causes countless bone spears to spring up from beneath the ground. Can impale multiple enemies simultaneously.

Seneijashu (Hidden Shadow Snake Hand): A technique used by Mitarashi Anko. She launches a surprise attack using snakes hidden in her sleeves. Snake techniques are said to be difficult, but since Anko was Orochimaru's pupil, perhaps she learnt it from him.

Sennengoroshi (lit. Death of a Thousand Years): The user steeples their index fingers, leaps into the air, and uses their entire body-weight to drive their fingers right into the opponent's...never mind.

Sensatsu Suisho (Thousand Flying Water Needles of Death): A tiny amount of water is turned into countless, sharp needles which are used to attack the enemy from all directions. One of Haku's favored techniques.

Sharingan (lit. Copy Wheel Eye): The Kekkeigenkai ability of the Uchiha Clan. It is a special eye that a very small percentage of the clan possesses. It gives them the power of insight, allowing them to see through illusions, and can be used to hypnotize others. Further, it allows its possessors to copy any techniques they see.

Shihohappo Shuriken (lit. Shuriken from All Directions): One of Naruto's techniques. Naruto creates Shadow Clones, and they all throw Shuriken simultaneously.

Shiki Fujin (Corpse Demon Seal Exhaustion): A last-ditch technique that seals the target's soul in Hell at the expense of the user's life. The fourth Lord Hokage uses it to seal away the Fox Spirit. The third also uses it during the fight with Orochimaru.

Shikokumujin (lit. Four Black Fog Battle Formation): Kekkai Ninjutsu in which the Oto no Yoninshu (Sound 4), surround the target and simultaneously place seals, trapping the victim in a cloud of black mist.

Shikomishindan (lit. Prepared Needle Shot): The user launches five

Senbon (needles) at their enemy from a concealed arm-mounted launcher. The needles are coated in poison which paralyzes the victim.

Shikon no Jutsu (lit. Dead Soul Technique): Ninjutsu that can temporarily revive a corpse's heart and allow it to be controlled using Chakra. This is Kabuto's specialty.

Shikotsumyaku (lit. Corpse Bone Pulse): The Kekkeigenkai ability of the Kaguya clan. Those who possess it can alter their own bone structure at will.

Shikyaku no Jutsu (lit. Four Legs Technique): One type of Giju Ninpo (lit. Beast Imitation Technique) used by Inuzukai Kiba.

Shinranshin no Jutsu (lit. Mind Body Disturbance Technique): The user projects their Chakra, taking control of the target. Unlike Shintenshin no Jutsu, the user is not left defenseless.

Shintenshin no Jutsu (lit. Mind Body Switch Technique): The user's psyche is projected onto that of the target, allowing the user to possess the target. However, the user's body is left defenseless during this time.

Shishi Rendan (Lion Combo): One of Sasuke's techniques. A high-speed combo requiring a high level of physical awareness. While in midair, Sasuke performs the Kage Buyo technique, follows with a flurry of punches and kicks, then uses the momentum to flip himself around and land a finishing kick. Because the target is already falling, the kicks serve to accelerate them, while the final kick delivers the coup de grace, slamming the victim to the ground for additional damage.

Shishienjin (lit. Four Violet Flames Battle Encampment): A powerful Oto no Yoninshu cooperative barrier technique. The four Oto no Yoninshu cast a Jutsu from four directions, creating a cube-shaped barrier. Anyone who touches the barrier immediately bursts into flames.

Shisho Fuin (Four Symbols Seal): A seal, used primarily to trap powerful spirits. A high level of ability is required to master it. Naruto's Hakke no Fuin Shiki consists of two of these.

Shosen Jutsu (lit. Enchanted Palm Technique): A medical Jutsu that dramatically improves recovery speed by sending Chakra through the palms into the wound or injured area. The amount of Chakra used must be controlled so that it is appropriate to the extent of the injury, this is a high-level technique that only a few medical Ninja can use.

Shunshin no Jutsu (lit. Body Flicker Technique): An instantaneous movement technique that allows the user to appear and disappear at will. It looks like teleportation, but in fact the technique uses Chakra to allow the user to move faster than the eye can see.

Shuriken Kage Bunshin no Jutsu (lit. Shuriken Shadow Clone Technique): The user applies the Kage Bunshin (shadow clone) technique to their Shuriken. This can cause one Shuriken to multiply into a thousand, doing more damage to the enemy. It is more difficult to use the Kage Bunshin technique on a physical object than on oneself. This technique was invented by the third Lord Hokage.

Shushagan no Jutsu (lit. Vanishing Face Copy Technique): Allows the user to steal the target's face and use it as their own. Since the target's face need only be touched, the user can obtain new disguises instantly. A technique used frequently by Orochimaru.

Sofushasan no Tachi (lit. Guided Windmill Triple Blades): First a Shuriken is thrown, followed by Kunai attached to cords. A tree or other object is used to allow the Shuriken to be returned with a yoyo-like motion. This is used to trick the opponent, as the Shuriken hits on its return swing.

Sojasosai no Jutsu (lit. Twin Snake Double Death): A forbidden technique Anko learns from Orochimaru. It is performed by binding the user's and opponent's hands with a single seal. If performed correctly, both user and target die.

Soma no Ko (lit. Double Demon Attack): A technique used by Ukon, who lives inside of his brother Sakon. The technique uses Ukon's ability to move around freely inside of Sakon during battle. Ukon can project his limbs or head out of any part of Sakon's body, allowing him to attack in unexpected ways.

Soshuha (lit. Guided Attack Blades): User throws multiple Kunai blades, each of which is controlled with Chakra. The floating Kunai are direct toward enemies from their blind side.

Sozosaisei (lit. Creation Rebirth): A forbidden medical technique of unsurpassed power, and Tsunade's most advanced regeneration technique. It greatly accelerates cell division in the body, speedy up healing so that even normally fatal wounds mend in an instant. However, this technique shortens the life of the person who performs it.

Suiro no Jutsu (lit. Water Prison Technique): Confines the target inside a sphere of water. It is impossible to dispel it from the inside. However, the user must remain in physical contact with the sphere to maintain it, leaving him or her open to attack from other enemies.

Suiton: Daibakufu no Jutsu (Water Release: Great Waterfall Technique): The user propels wide area of water several tens of meters into the air, and drops it on the target like a massive waterfall. The effect is like that of a tidal wave

Suiton: Suikodan no Jutsu (lit. Water Release: Water Shark Bullet Technique): The user propels a huge volume of water into the air, and brings it down on the opponent.

Suiton: Suigadan (lit. Water Release: Water Fang Bullet): The user hits the target with a spinning mass of water, doing physical damage.

Suiton: Suijinheki (lit. Water Release: Water Encampment Wall): A technique in which the user shapes water into a wall by beating it violently in order to block enemy attacks. The defense creates a 360 degree barrier, blocking attacks from any direction.

Suiton: Suiryudan no Jutsu (lit. Water Release: Water Dragon Bullet Technique): A technique that inflicts physical damage by battering the target with a large amount of water with overwhelming force. The water, under the control of the user, takes on the form of a dragon, hence the name.

Suiton: Teppodama (Water Release: Gunshot): A technique used by Gamabunta. He transforms his Chakra into a ball of water and spits it.

Suna Bunshin (lit. Sand Clone): A technique used by Gaara. Gaara can create a copy of himself made of congealed sand. Unlike regular clones, the sand clone can change its form, for example stretching out its arm to strike a distant opponent.

Suna no Tate (Shield of Sand): The sand Gaara carries around in his gourd will autonomously form a shield protecting him from attack, whether he likes it or not.

Suna no Yoroi (lit. Armor of Sand): A defensive technique used by Gaara. Gaara's body is surrounded by sand, which serves as armor to protect his body from any attack.

Suna Shigure (lit. Sand Drizzle): Pelts the target from every direction with pebbles of compacted sand.

T

Taju Kage Bunshin no Jutsu (lit. Multiple Shadow Clone Technique): Creates Shadow Clones, which unlike illusory clones have a physical presence. Each clone then performs the Shadow Clone technique, creating a huge number of clones. Because this technique uses a huge amount of Chakra, it can only be performed by those with Naruto's level of stamina.

Tanuki Neiri no Jutsu (lit. Tanuki Sleep Technique): Gaara uses a form of self-hypnosis to put himself to sleep, allowing him access to Shukaku's power. Since Gaara himself loses consciousness, Shukaku controls his actions.

Tarenken (lit. Multiple Connected Punches): Combination attack used by Sakon and Ukon. They use their four arms to beat down opponents.

Tarenkyaku (lit. Multiple Connected Kicks) : An attack used by Sakon and Ukon. Ukon fuses both of his legs to Sakon's leg when he delivers a kick, increasing the kicking leg's weight and power.

Teshi Sendan (lit. Finger Bullet Drill): One of Kimimaro's techniques. Allows him to eject pieces of bone from his fingertips and shoot them at his enemies.

Tessenka no Mai: Hana (lit. Dance of the Clematis: Flower): One of Kimimaro's techniques. The Shikotsumyaku is performed with a huge amount of Chakra to create a spear of the utmost hardness. The opponent is immobilized with Tessenka no Mai: Tsuru, making it impossible to avoid the spear attack.

Tessenka no Mai: Tsuru (lit. Dance of the Clematis: Vine): One of Kimimaro's techniques. Allows him to use his own spinal cord as a whip and tie up opponents.

Tomegane no Jutsu (lit. Telescope Technique): A technique that allows the user to watch a specific person through a crystal ball. The Chakra pattern of that person must be known in advance to perform it.

Tsubaki no Mai (lit. Dance of the Camellia): One of Kimimaro's techniques. He wields a sword, created from his own bones, at speeds to fast for the eye to see. The after-image of his sword on the retina creates the illusion of many swords.

Tsuga (lit. Piercing Fang): One of Kiba's techniques. Kiba spins his body at high speed to maximize his attack's power and penetration.

Tsukuyomi (lit. Moon Reader): An extreme form of Genjutsu that only possessors of the Mangekyo Sharingan can use. Puts victims in their own private Hell, which exists in the mind of the user.

Tsutenkyaku (lit. Painful Sky Leg): One of Tsunade's techniques. She raises one leg and brings her heel down with all her might.

U

Urarenge (lit. Reverse Lotus): A technique used by Lee and Guy. The "eight gates" that limit Chakra within the body are opened, allowing the user to attack with superhuman speed; it is Lee's ultimate weapon.

Uzumaki Naruto Rendan (lit. Uzumaki Naruto Combo): An original Ninjutsu created by Naruto. He creates four Shadow Clones, who shout "U! Zu! Ma! Ki!" while kicking their opponent into the air. While the opponent is still sailing through the air helpless, Naruto delivers a final devastating kick.

Z

Zankuha (lit. Decapitating Air Wave): One of Zaku Abumi's techniques; he can release controlled bursts of energy composed of air-pressure or supersonic waves from the vents in his arms. If he uses a higher ratio of air-pressure, the blast can crush rocks. If he uses more ultrasound, he can make the ground soft and spongy.

Zesshi Nensan (lit. Tongue Tooth Sticky Acid): The name of a viscous fluid Katsuyu spits. It is acidic, and corrosive enough to vaporize rocks in seconds.

Zankukyokuha (lit. Extreme Decapitating Air Waves): A more powerful version of Zaku Abumi's Zankuha technique that allows him to utilize air-pressure or supersonic waves fired from the vents in his arms. The technique consumes a lot of Chakra, but causes massive destruction to a large area. Since it puts a lot of stress on his arms, he can't use it too often.

GLOSSARY

A

Aburame Clan: A clan from Konohagakure that uses insects.

Akatsuki: A mysterious group composed of nine Ninja. All nine are wanted S-rank felons. Orochimaru is a former member.

Akimichi Clan: A clan from Konohagakure that uses the Baika no Jutsu.

Anbu: Abbreviation of Ansatsu Senjutsu Tokushu Butai (lit. Assassination Warfare Special Force). Task force that engages in assassinations and espionage.

B

Bingo Book: A small, heavily guarded book containing details on particularly dangerous people - for example those who have attempted to start insurrections or committed unauthorized assassinations. Each village has its own book.

C

Chakra: The source of the Ninja's power. Molded by the user's stamina, and which techniques they wish to use. It is closely related to the Ninja's physical and psychological strength, so the potential for increasing Chakra is directly proportional to the talent of the Ninja.

Chidori (lit. Thousand Birds): Technique created by Kakashi upon obtaining his Jonin rank. It can be performed quickly with no wasted effort.

Chunin (lit. Middle Ninja): The officers of the Ninja hierarchy. Ninja must pass the Chunin exams to progress to this class.

Chunin Exams: Selection exam for Genin wishing to progress to Chunin; held jointly by the allied nations twice a year.

Copy Ninja: Hatake Kakashi's nickname. He is called this because he has used his Sharingan to copy over a thousand techniques from Ninja he's met.

D

Daisanji Ninkai Taisen (Third Great Ninja War): A huge war that occurred between the villages of the Five Great Countries. An epic battle between Konohagakure and Iwagakure ensued.

Densetsu no Kamo (Sitting Duck): Refers to Tsunade, who loves gambling and frequents gambling establishments everywhere she goes, but never seems to win.

Densetsu no Sannin (the Legendary Three Ninja): Three powerful Ninja from the village of Konohagakure: Jiraiya, Orochimaru and Tsunade.

F

Five Great Countries: The five countries containing the five Shinobi villages: the Land of Earth (Iwagakure), the Land of Fire (Konohagakure), Land of Thunder (Kumogakure), the Land of Water (Kirigakure), and the Land of Wind (Sunagakure).

Fuin no Sho (lit. Book of Seals) : A scroll containing seals deemed dangerous by the first Lord Hokage. Contains forbidden techniques, such as the Multiple Shadow Clone Technique.

Fuinjutsu (lit. Seal Technique): Techniques used to seal away evil spirits or the effects of curse seals.

G

Gato Company: Shipping company run by the crime lord Gato.

Genin (lit. Lower Ninja): The lowest and most common rank of Ninja. Ninja who graduate from the Ninja Academy start out at this rank.

Genjutsu (lit. Illusion Technique): Refers to all psychological techniques used by Ninja, including illusions and hypnosis.

Goikenban (lit. Advisory Council): A council of elders, who use their accumulated wisdom and experience to assist the Hokage and guide village policy.

Gokage (lit. Five Shadows): Generic term for the leaders of the Ninja villages of the Five Great Countries: Hokage, Mizukage, Kazekage, Tsuchikage and Raikage.

Goken (lit. Strong Fist): A Taijutsu (fighting style based on direct, physical attacks) that focuses on dealing out external damage. It is distinguished from Juken, which is used to cause internal damage.

H

Hachimon Tonko no Tainaimon: The eight secret "gates" of the pressure point system through which Chakra flows. Because these points regulate the flow of Chakra, if they are opened the user temporarily receives a massive amount of power and superhuman abilities. However, it places a tremendous strain on the body.

Hiden (lit. Secret): Secret techniques unique to the region, and passed on by oral tradition.

Hitaiate: The term for the headband given to Ninja when the graduate from Ninja Academy. Each village's headband bears the symbol for that village.

Hyorogan (Soldier Pill): Small capsule that contains various nutrients. Just one pill allows the Ninja to go for three days and nights with no food, drink or sleep.

Hyuga Clan: The oldest clan in Konohagakure, and incidentally the clan with the best land. This clan posses the hereditary Byakugan ability.

I

Iryohan (lit. Medical Unit): A group of medical specialists. Membership is limited to Ninja who use medical techniques.

J

Jugen (Gentle Fist): A kind of Taijutsu; as opposed to Goken (Strong Fist), it aims to cause internal, rather than external damage. .

Juinjustu (Cursed Seal Techniques): A curse technique used to draw out evil spirits, control actions, or control oneself. Markings appear on the neck and face of those with a Cursed Seal.

Jonin (lit. Elite Ninja): Rank reached by Ninja after they progress through the Genin and Chunin levels. Jonin is the top class. Very few Ninja reach this class. Those who do are practically superhuman in their own right.

K

Kaguya Clan: Clan that possesses the hereditary Shikotsumyaku ability. A warlike and foolhardy clan, they sow the seeds of their own ruin by trying to stage a coup of Kirigakure village.

Kaoiwa (lit. Face Rock): Cliff that dominates the scenery of Konohagakure; has the faces of the successive Lords Hokage carved into it.

Karasu: Puppet used by Kankuro of Sunagakure. Designed for battle, and armed with various weapons.

Katatein (lit. One-handed Seal): Seal that only requires one hand to perform (most techniques require both hands).

Kekkeigenkai (lit. Bloodline Limit): Special genetic abilities. The Uchiha Clan's Sharingan and the Kaguya Clan's Shikotsumyaku are examples of this phenomenon.

Kibaku Fuda (lit. Exploding Tag): A tool used by Ninja. Consists of a tag with a timed explosion formula written on it. If the tag is affixed to something, it will explode when the appointed time arrives.

Kikaichu (Destruction Bugs): Insects that feed off Chakra. The Aburame Clan host the bugs within their own bodies.

Kinjutsu (lit. forbidden technique): Techniques which are forbidden to Ninja because they pose too great a strain on the user, or are too immoral.

Kirigakure: A mist-enshrouded village located to the East of Konohagakure. Located within the Land of Water.

Kirigakure no Kaijin (lit. Stranger of Kirigakure): Another name for Hoshigaki Kisame, who is a member of Akatsuki.

Kirigakure no Kijin (lit. Demon of Kirigakure): Another name for Zabuza. He earned this nickname by slaughtering 100 of his peers during the Kirigakure graduation exams.

Kiri no Shinobigatana no

Shichininshu (lit. Seven Ninja Blades of Kirigakure): The seven Ninja who formerly made up the core of Kirigakure's military power. They were called this because they all used swords.

Konohagakure: Shinobi village ruled by the Lord Hokage. Located in the Land of Fire. Naruto is from this village.

Konoha Kuzushi (Breaking the Konoha): The coup staged by Orochimaru. He tried to use the Chunin exams to execute his plan.

Konoha no Kiroi Senko (lit. Konoha's Yellow Flash): The fourth Lord Hokage's nickname.

Konoha no Shiroi Kiba (lit. White Fang of Konoha): Nickname of Hatake Sakumo (Hatake Kakashi's father) so-called because he carried a bright, short blade into battle.

Konoha Police: Organization that keeps public order in Konoha. For generations, the Uchiha Clan has headed this group.

Kubikiri Hocho (lit. Beheading Knife): Zabuza's weapon of choice. The blade is over two meters long and weighs upwards of 30 kilograms. Despite its size, Zabuza has no trouble wielding it.

Kunai: A tool used by Ninja. These small knives have little stopping power, but their light weight and flexibility makes them popular with Ninja.

Kusanagi no Tsurugi (lit. Grass Cutter): Orochimaru's sword. In Japanese mythology, there is also a blade by this name that was said to be made of the tail of a huge, eight-headed serpent named Orochi.

Kyodai Sensu (lit. Great Fan): Giant folding fan that Temari, a Ninja from Sunagakure, uses as her weapon. The fan is as big as she is, and produces violent gusts of wind.

M

Make-out Paradise: Jiraiya's adult-oriented novel. Kakashi is a big fan of the book.

Make-Out Violence: The sequel to Jiraiya's best-seller, Icha Icha Paradaisu.

Makibishi (Caltrop): A tool used by Ninja. Consist of sharpened barbs. They are scattered in the path of enemies to slow them down.

N

Naruto Ohashi (Great Naruto Bridge): The name given to the great bridge built by Tazuna, who overcame many hardships to connect the Land of Waves with the mainland. Named in honor of Naruto, whose courage made the completion of the bridge possible.

Ningu (lit. Ninja Tool): Any weapon, protective gear etc. used by Ninja.

Ninja Academy: An institution that trains Ninja. Those who graduate from it are registered as Ninja. .

Ninja Torokusho (Ninja Registry): A license Ninja carry to prove they are qualified to perform their duties. Because an accurate assessment of potential military strength is important to the villages, these licenses are managed very carefully.

Ninjutsu: Refers mainly to techniques in which Chakra is used. There are many types of Ninjutsu, including those focused on attack, espionage and defense.

Ninken (Ninja Dogs): These dogs are specially trained and have learned some Ninjutsu, allowing them to support the Ninja during their operations. The Inuzukai Clan particularly adept at training the Ninja Dogs. Hatake Kakashi is a specialist in the use of the Ninken, and can summon up to eight at once using Kuchiyose.

Nukenin (Missing-Nin): Ninja who abscond from their villages as deserters or traitors. Because these Ninja are privy to their village's secret Ninjutsu, they usually become the targets of Oinin assassinations.

O

Oinin (Hunter-Nin): Specialist Ninja who assassinate Nukenin (Missing-Nin). Actually, they don't just assassinate them; they eradicate all traces of the bodies too.

Otogakure: A village recently created by Orochimaru (originally from Konohagakure).

P

Professor: Another name for the third Lord Hokage. He earned this title due to his passion for learning, which lead him to research and master all the techniques of the village. He was also called the "God of Shinobi" and considered the most powerful

Lord Hokage in the history of the village.

R

Ramen Ichiraku: Naruto's favorite ramen shop. The shop's delicious pork soup and ornery owner are famous.

S

Samehada (lit. Sharkskin): Hoshigaki Kisame's blade. Destroys its victim's Chakra.

Sanshoku no Ganyaku (lit. Three Colored Pills): A secret supplement devised by the Akimichi clan. Comes in curry, spinach and chili pepper flavors. Each dose provides a burst of power.

Seals: Formed with the finger when invoking techniques. Vary depending on what technique is being invoked.

Senbon (Needle): A tool used by Ninja. A large needle, with not much killing power. It can also be used to perform healing acupuncture.

Shinobigashira (lit. Head of the Shinobi): A position even higher than Jonin; part of the village's Ninja army.

Shi no Mori (Forest of Death): Another name for the practice areas located on the fringes of Konohagakure. Site of the second stage of the Chunin exam.

Shuriken: The most well known member of the Ninja's arsenal. It is essentially a star-shaped blade. Usually thrown. It was used more for distraction than actual killing.

Silent Killing: Zabuza's favored assassination technique. He blinds the target with mist, then strikes

Smoke Bomb: A tool used by Ninja. A round pellet made of special materials that produces clouds of smoke when thrown. Used as a diversion.

Sunagakure: A Shinobi village located to the West of Konohagakure. Located within the Land of Wind. Led by Lord Kazekage. Gaara and Kankuro are from this village

Suna no Keshin (lit. Incarnation of Sand): The spirit Shukaku that is sealed within Gaara.

T

Taijutsu (lit. Body Techniques): Refers to all direct, physical techniques used by Ninja, including punches and kicks.

Tanzakugai: A large entertainment district in the East part of the Land of Fire. Contains numerous gambling houses, bars and amusement centers. .

Tanzakujo (lit. Tanzaku Castle) : The old castle standing in the center of Tanzaku. Designated as a "cultural asset" by the Land of Fire. Reduced to rubble by Orochimaru.. .

Tenketsu (Pressure Points) : The 361 pressure points on the body. Chakra flows through these points. By accurately hitting these points, one can stop the flow of Chakra in one's opponent

Ten no Sho, Chi no Sho (Book of Heaven, Book of Earth): The scroll used in the second stage of the Chunin exam. Each team was given one or the other, and had to steal whichever one they did not have from another team..

Tokubetsu Jonin (lit. Special Elite Ninja): Ninja specially assigned due to their skills in torture, assassination, espionage etc. Their rank is higher than Chunin, but lower than Jonin.

U

Uchiha Clan : Clan from Konohagakure that possess the Sharingan.

Z

Zettai Bogyo (lit. Absolute Defense): 1. Refers to the Suna no Tate (Shield of Sand) and Suna no Yoroi (Armor of Sand), which make up Gaara's perfect defense.. 2. The ability to dodge any attack from any angle, a power bestowed by the Byakugan.

KEYWORD INDEX

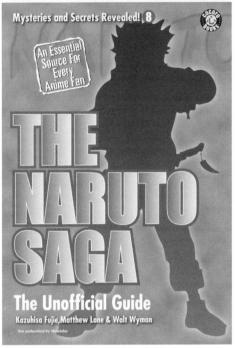